Ireland

by Penny Phenix

Penny Phenix has many years of experience in
writing and editing travel guides, and has
specialised in books about Britain and Ireland.
She is the author of a number of AA books,
including *Explore Britain's Historic Houses* and
the AA/OS *Leisure Guide Devon*, and has
contributed to other publications, including
Interactive Britain & Ireland (CD-ROM).

Arthurstown, Ballyhack harbour and castle, Co Wexford

AA Publishing

A nun in Killarney

Written by Penny Phenix. Updated by Anita Heffernan
© Automobile Association Developments Limited 1998
First published 1998.
Reprinted 2001. Information verified and updated.
Reprinted 2003. Reprinted 2004 with amendments.
Reprinted May 2004.
Reprinted 2005. Information verified and updated.
Reprinted May and Aug 2005
Reprinted 2007. Information verified and updated.

Automobile Association Developments Limited retains the
copyright in the original edition © 1998
Published and distributed in the United Kingdom by
AA Publishing, a trading name of Automobile Association
Developments Limited, whose registered office is Fanum
House, Basing View, Basingstoke, Hampshire, REG21 4EA
Registered number 1878835.

® Northern Ireland mapping reproduced by
permission of the Ordnance Survey of
Northern Ireland on behalf of the Controller
ORDNANCE SURVEY® of Her Majesty's Stationery Office
OF NORTHERN IRELAND © Crown copyright 2006, Permit No. 60026.
Republic of Ireland mapping based on Ordnance Survey Ireland
Permit No. 8136. © Ordnance Survey Ireland and Government
of Ireland.

Mapping produced by the Cartographic Department of the
Automobile Association.

A CIP catalogue record for this book is available from the
British Library.

Colour separation by Keenes in Andover
Printed and bound in Italy by Printer Trento S.r.l

A03021

Find out more about
AA Publishing and the
wide range of travel
publications and services
the AA provides by
visiting our website at
www.theAA.com/travel

Contents

About this Book

KEY TO SYMBOLS

➕ map reference to the maps found in the What to See section

✉ address or location

☎ telephone number

🕓 opening times

🍴 restaurant or café on premises or near by

Ⓜ nearest underground train station

🚌 nearest bus/tram route

🚉 nearest overground train station

⛴ ferry crossings and boat excursions

✈ travel by air

ℹ tourist information

♿ facilities for visitors with disabilities

👆 admission charge

↔ other places of interest near by

❓ other practical information

➤ indicates the page where you will find a fuller description

This book is divided into five sections to cover the most important aspects of your visit to the island.

Viewing Ireland pages 5–14
An introduction to Ireland by the author.
Ireland's Features
Essence of Ireland
The Shaping of Ireland
Peace and Quiet
Ireland's Famous

Top Ten pages 15–26
The author's choice of the Top Ten places to see on the islands, listed in alphabetical order, each with practical information.

What to See pages 27–90
The four main areas of Ireland, each with its own brief introduction and an alphabetical listing of the main attractions.
Practical information
Snippets of 'Did you know…' information
4 suggested walks
4 suggested tours
3 features

Where To... pages 91–116
Detailed listings of the best places to eat, stay, shop, take the children and be entertained.

Practical Matters pages 117–24
A highly visual section containing essential travel information.

Maps
All map references are to the individual maps found in the What to See section of this guide.
For example, Dublin Castle has the reference ➕ 36B3 – indicating the page on which the map is located and the grid square in which the castle is to be found. A list of the maps that have been used in this travel guide can be found in the index.

Prices
Where appropriate, an indication of the cost of an establishment is given by € signs:

€€€ denotes higher prices, €€ denotes average prices, while € denotes lower charges.

Star Ratings
Most of the places described in this book have been given a separate rating:

😀😀😀 Do not miss
😀😀 Highly recommended
😀 Worth seeing

Viewing Ireland

Above: *Dan Foley's Pub, Anascaul,
Co Kerry*
Right: *girl with piglet at Dingle Farm,
Peninsula World*

Penny Phenix's Ireland

A Gentler Pace

Ireland is famous for its relaxed pace of life, and even in the cities, where there is much activity, there is an overall feeling that anything that can't be achieved today can easily wait until tomorrow. An Irishman was once asked if there was an equivalent Irish word for *mañana*. 'Oh no', he replied, 'we have nothing with that sense of urgency!'

Traditional and Informal

Traditional music sessions are widespread throughout Ireland. Some city pubs will have them every night, with different musicians at each, and even in the country there will be a session somewhere within easy reach. Sessions are informal and unrehearsed, but the fiddlers, flautists, whistlers, pipers, *bodhrán* players and whoever else may turn up all know the tunes and standards are very high.

Sheltered Strangford Lough in County Down is perfect for weekend sailing

I first visited Ireland in the 1980s, when I was offered the use of a cottage on the southwest coast, overlooking Dunmanus Bay. It was absolutely magical – the view from the cottage was magnificent, seals would pop their heads above water (just a few feet away) to greet me as I looked out of the bedroom window in the morning, the locals were delightful and we made lots of friends in the tiny corrugated iron shack that served as the local bar.

At the same time I found an undercurrent of sadness at the ailing economy and the rampant depopulation, particularly among the young. Many properties were being snapped up by outsiders for use as holiday homes, which would stand empty for much of the year.

Since that first visit I have travelled the length and breadth of the island and been charmed by it all. I would certainly urge anyone not to be deterred from visiting Northern Ireland, where the sporadic hostilities are far outweighed by the friendliness of the majority of the population, the beautiful scenery, historic buildings and cultural activities.

Visiting the Republic these days I find that the magic in the scenery and the genuinely welcoming people remains unchanged. But where there was concern for the future there is now great optimism. EU membership has turned the economy round, the flow of emigration has reversed and areas that were once down-at-heel are regenerating. Ireland has its own way of combining prosperity and progress with tradition and a relaxed attitude to life. As of old, nothing is so urgent that it should stand in the way of a good conversation with someone you have only just met.

Ireland's Features

Geographical Information
• Ireland lies on the continental shelf to the west of the European mainland. To the east, over the Irish Sea, lies Britain, with Scotland 21km to the northeast.
• In area Ireland is 7 million hectares and of those hectares 2.25 million are devoted to agriculture.
• The largest county is Cork and the smallest is Louth.
• The highest mountain is Carrantuohill, 1,041m, in the Macgillicuddy's Reeks range of Co Kerry.
• The longest river is the Shannon at 340km, while the largest lake is Lough Neagh at 396sq km.
• Rainfall on the west coast averages 1300mm (but can exceed 2000mm in mountain areas). On the east coast, in the driest area near Dublin, the maximum is 750mm.

Sport and Leisure
• Salmon season: January to September.
• Brown trout season: 15 February to 12 October.
• Sea trout fishing: June to September (or 12 October in some places).
• There is no close season for coarse fishing, and sea angling is possible all year round, depending upon weather conditions.
• Ireland has over 11,000 pubs.
• There are over 400 golf courses in Ireland.

Famous Products
• **Alcohol** Bushmills, Jameson, Powers and Paddy whiskeys; Guinness, Beamish and Murphy's stout, Smithwick's beer; Cork gin; Baileys liqueur.
• **Irish Linen** Banbridge Co Down is the main centre. The Ferguson Linen Centre has factory tours, and Banbridge is the starting point of Linen Tours, a coach journey around nearby sites, including linen mills and factories. There is also an Irish Linen Centre in Lisburn.

• **Donegal Tweed** Magee & Co in Donegal town have been manufacturing tweed since 1866; Ardara Heritage Centre tells the story of Donegal tweed and Aran knitwear, and there are tours of hand-loom weaving centres.
• **Aran Sweaters** The distinctive patterns of the traditional Aran sweater are known all over the world. They are still produced in the Aran Islands.
• **Waterford Crystal** Waterford Crystal is widely available throughout Ireland (and the world). The factory has organised tours (➤ 58).
• **Racehorses** Irish-bred racehorses are prized all over the world. Kildare is at the heart of horse-racing country and home of the National Stud. The great plain of The Curragh, stretching away to the west of the town, is dotted with stud farms, many in international ownership.

Ireland's most popular product dominates this Dublin scene

Animal Life
• There are over 55,000 horses in Ireland, of which some 15,000 are racehorses.
• Ireland has 27 mammal species, but only one reptile, the common lizard.
• There are no moles in Ireland.
• There are around 125 species of resident wild birds in Ireland, and 250 species of visiting birds.

Essence of Ireland

If your time in Ireland is limited you will need to be selective, and one of the best ways of making your selections is by asking the locals. The conversations that will inevitably ensue will be as rewarding as the information you will glean. The essence of Ireland and the friendly good humour of the Irish people are inextricably linked.

Blakes Bar in Enniskillen is typical of Ireland's atmospheric town pubs

Ireland has great cities in each of its four quarters – Dublin in the east, Belfast in the north, Limerick and Galway in the west and Cork in the south – and just a short visit to each will demonstrate the differences in character between these regions.

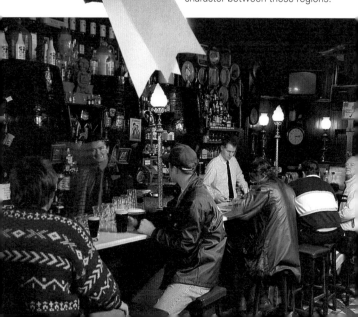

THE **10** ESSENTIALS

If you only have a short time to visit Ireland, or would like to get a really complete picture of the country, here are the essentials:

• **Drive the Ring of Kerry** (▶ 54) to see some of Ireland's most spectacular coastal and inland scenery, including huge fjord-like bays, the country's highest mountain, sparkling lakes, pretty villages and colourful hedgerows and gardens, which flourish in an exceptionally mild climate.

• **Join in a *ceilí*,** with traditional music and dancing to sweep you on to your feet.

• **Wander along Grafton Street in Dublin,** for the shops and the buskers, and have a coffee at Bewley's Café, a great Dublin institution, on the way.

• **Go to a race meeting at The Curragh.** The Irish have

the millions of emigrants who left this beautiful country for an unknown destiny in the New World.

• **Visit Skibbereen on the day of the cattle market** to sample the real working life of an agricultural community, but do not be in a hurry on the road because you will be following all manner of vehicles bringing livestock into town – all part of the experience.

• **For a taste of Ireland, eat oysters and drink Guinness** at Paddy Burke's Oyster Inn in Clarenbridge, Co Galway, famous for its oyster festival. To experience the

a unique affinity with horses and a day at the races here is quite an experience.

• **Visit Glendalough** to soak up the atmosphere of this historic ruined monastic city in a beautiful valley of the Wicklow Mountains.

• **Look out from the Cliffs of Moher,** with no other landfall between here and North America, and contemplate the feelings of

oyster festival, visit Clarenbridge in September.

• **Rent a cruiser and explore the lovely River Shannon,** its lakes and the historic sites, riverside towns and villages along the way.

• **Take a walk along the clifftops of Co Antrim to the Giant's Causeway** to see how ancient travellers would have first witnessed this most remarkable place.

Art and humour combine on this wall in Lisdoonvarna, Co Clare

The Shaping of Ireland

8000 BC
First settlement by hunters and fishermen.

4000 BC
The farming Gaels arrive and the Celtic language develops.

AD 350
Christianity reaches Ireland.

AD 432
St Patrick arrives in Ireland to begin his mission to convert the population to Christianity. The next three centuries see the foundation of many of Ireland's greatest monasteries and the production of wonderful illuminated manuscripts including the famous *Book of Kells* and the *Book of Durrow*, both now in Trinity College Library in Dublin.

795
The Vikings invade Ireland, establish settlements at Dublin, Waterford and other coastal towns and introduce trade and the first coinage.

1014
High King of Ireland, Brian Ború, vanquishes the Vikings, but dies before he can achieve his aim of uniting Ireland.

1169
Ousted king Dermot MacMurrough invites the Anglo-Normans to help him regain his throne. They grasp the opportunity, and seize Ireland for themselves.

1541
Henry VIII forces Irish chiefs to surrender their land.

1558–1603
Elizabeth I tightens English hold on Ireland and establishes English and Scottish immigrants on land expropriated from the native Irish.

1595–1603
Rebellion led by Hugh O'Neill, Earl of Tyrone, fails after the Battle of Kinsale, resulting in the Flight of the Earls (Irish aristocracy) to Europe.

1649
Oliver Cromwell conducts an aggressive campaign to impose his religion on the Irish, during which thousands of Irish are massacred. Cromwell's opponents have their land seized.

The capture of Wolfe Tone, the 18th-century revolutionary leader

1689
James II of England flees to Ireland after being deposed. He is finally defeated at the Battle of the Boyne by William of Orange, who became William III of England.

1691
The Treaty of Limerick heralds the ascendancy of the Protestant minority.

1704
Penal Code introduced, which restricts Catholic landowning and bans Catholics from voting, attending schools and military service.

1782
Ireland allowed its own parliament and a period of greater religious tolerance ensues.

1798
Wolfe Tone leads United Irishmen in an uprising, which is crushed.

1800
Ireland becomes part of Britain under the Act of Union.

1845–8
The Potato Famine and widespread emigration reduces the population by 2 million.

1916
The Easter Rising leads to the execution of 16 leaders of the Irish Republican Brotherhood.

1920–1
Creation of the Irish Free State and separation of

The cover of a momentous special issue of Irish Life

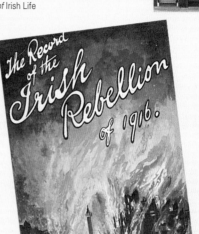

Northern Ireland (Ulster), resulting in Civil War over the Anglo-Irish Treaty.

1949
Creation of the Republic of Ireland (Eire).

1969
The Troubles begin in Northern Ireland. British troops are called in after riots in Londonderry. The Provisional IRA launches a campaign of violence.

1972
The Republic joins the EEC (EU).

1974
Breakdown of Northern Irish Assembly leads to direct rule from London.

1985
Anglo-Irish Agreement gives Republic of Ireland some involvement in Northern Irish affairs.

1998
Good Friday Agreement creates a new Northern Ireland Assembly.

2000
Urban regeneration projects underway in Dublin and Belfast.

2002
The Republic adopts the euro as its currency.

2004
In March a non-smoking law is introduced in all enclosed public places.

11

Peace & Quiet

Getting away from it all in Ireland is not a difficult thing to do. Even from the centres of its largest towns and cities there are tantalising glimpses of remote hilltops, and within a half-hour drive of Dublin or Belfast you could be standing in complete isolation, surrounded by some of the most beautiful scenery in the country.

The beach at Cougher on the Dingle Peninsula

Around the Coast

Ireland has some of Europe's emptiest and cleanest beaches, with great expanses of silvery sands and little rocky coves. The Donegal coast is renowned for its wonderful beaches, such as those at Bundoran, Creeslough, Fintragh Bay, Portnoo and Rathmullan. In Sligo those at Enniscrone, Mullaghmore and Rosses Point are among the best, while the south has the huge Barley Cove and fine beaches around Youghal. Swathes of sand stretch all along the east coast, and in the north Benone Strand extends for 11km, backed by cliffs and dunes. Cranfield Beach, south of Kilkeel, is said to have the warmest water in the north.

Birdwatchers head for the great river estuaries, such as Strangford Lough, near Belfast, and the Shannon estuary in the west, where the mudflats are teeming with feeding birds. Offshore islands offer the most exciting sightings, particularly Rathlin Island in the north, the Saltee Islands off the southeastern corner and Cape Clear in the southwest. And do not miss the Cliffs of Moher (➤ 67).

Inland Waterways

There are thousands of lakes in Ireland, particularly in the 'lakeland counties' which extend southwards from the border with Northern Ireland and in Connemara. Lough Neagh in Northern Ireland is the largest lake of all, and contains two fish which are almost exclusive to these waters – the pollan and the dollaghan. The wide rivers Erne and Shannon, which widen even further into

beautiful lakes as they flow seaward, are popular for cruiser holidays, and all of Ireland's lovely rivers are tranquil.

National Parks and Forest Parks

The large number of nature reserves all over Ireland are rich in animal and plant life, and the national parks preserve some large areas of great beauty. Killarney National Park includes the most extensive areas of natural woodland remaining in Ireland. The Glenveagh National Park in Co Donegal consists of beautiful mountains, lakes, glens and woods, with a herd of red deer, and the Connemara National Park in Co Galway is very special.

There are great forest parks too, many with visitor centres, waymarked walks, scenic drives and picnic places. In Northern Ireland, Tollymore in the Mountains of Mourne, Castlewellan Forest Park and Gortin Glen in the Sperrin Mountains are particularly popular; in the Republic, Glengarriff Forest Park in the Beara Peninsula is among the finest, and the one near Rathdrum has one of Europe's finest collections of trees.

Gardens

Ireland's mild climate is a great boon to its gardeners, particularly in the west, where the Gulf Stream lengthens the flowering season and makes all kinds of things possible. The Sub-Tropical Gardens on Garinish Island off the Beara Peninsula (➤ 52) are a spectacular example. The stately homes of Ireland are enhanced by their gardens too. Those at Powerscourt, just south of Dublin, are among the finest in Europe, and in Northern Ireland Mount Stewart Gardens and Rowallane are exceptional among the National Trust's many properties there.

The attractive little town of Clifden is surrounded by spectacular Connemara scenery

Ireland's Famous

Words and Images

Irish subjects are increasingly attracting the film industry's moguls, including *The Crying Game*, *In the Name of the Father*, *Michael Collins* and *Angela's Ashes*, shot on location in Limerick. *The Field*, filmed at Leenane in Connemara in the early 1990s, starring Richard Harris and John Hurt, was a surprise success. Less famous, but offering a compelling insight into life in the west of Ireland, was *Man of Aran*, made by Irish-American director Robert Flaherty in 1934.

Blarney

Words have always been important to the Irish. Around the time of the birth of Christ, the Celts were described by the Greek geographer Strabo as being fond of 'wordy disputes' and 'bombastic self-dramatisation'. Later, in Elizabethan times, the Earl of Blarney so infuriated the queen with his lengthy but empty promises that she declared 'I will have no more of this Blarney talk', coining the phrase long before kissing the Blarney Stone came into vogue.

For a small country, Ireland has more than its fair share of exceptional talent. Few other countries of this size can boast of so many internationally recognised names.

Stage and Screen

Irish actors have for many years found much favour with the great studios of Hollywood and major stars include Liam Neeson, Gabriel Byrne, Daniel Day Lewis, Kenneth Branagh, Stephen Rea, Peter O'Toole and Richard Harris, not to mention countless Americans with Irish connections, such as Martin Sheen, whose mother came from Borrisokane in Co Tipperary.

Music

Many Irish musicians have found international recognition. Irish tenors were enormously popular in the early 20th century, and the names of Joseph Locke and John McCormick were known far beyond their native shores. The world of rock and pop music has also included a strong contingent of Irish bands and soloists, such as Bob Geldof's Boomtown Rats, Van Morrison, U2, The Cranberries, Boyzone, Enya, Sinéad O'Connor, The Corrs and Westlife. Traditional music has been taken all over the world by The Chieftains, and Riverdance, which showcases Irish traditional dance, continues to be an international success. In the realm of classical music, the flautist James Galway has international stature.

The World of Literature

Even before the written word, Ireland had a strong tradition of storytelling, and Irish writers are among the most acclaimed in the world. No fewer than four have received the Nobel Prize for Literature – W B Yeats, George Bernard Shaw, Samuel Beckett and Seamus Heaney. Many consider it surprising that Dubliner James Joyce did not receive the same recognition. Novelist Roddy Doyle is a Booker-prize winner and Frank McCourt won the Pulitzer for *Angela's Ashes*. Jonathan Swift and Oscar Wilde were both Irish, and Bram Stoker was born and raised in Dublin.

A bronze statue of James Joyce watches over the junction of O'Connell and Earl streets in Dublin

Top Ten

Above: *jaunting car at Muckross Estate*
Right: *cross at the sacred site of Clonmacnoise*

1
The Aran Islands

🕂 62A2

🚌 No public transport on the islands

✈ Aer Arann (☎ 091-593034; www.aerarannislands.ie) flights taking 10 minutes from Connemara Airport, Co Galway. May–Aug every 30 minutes (last flight 7PM); Sep–Apr less frequent

⛴ Island Ferries (☎ Galway: 091-568903, Rossaveal: 091-572050) operate several sailings daily from Rossaveal, Co Galway

Aran's Heritage Centre

✉ Kilronan, Inis Mór

☎ 099-61355

🕐 Jun–Aug daily 10–7; Apr–May, Sep–Oct daily 11–5

✋ Cheap

The bleak Inis Mór coast

Bleak and virtually treeless, these three remote islands on the very edge of Europe have a fascinating cultural heritage.

From the mainland, the distant sight of the three Aran Islands is mysterious and inviting. The west coast of Ireland may seem a remote outpost of Europe, and yet here is something beyond – a place where Gaelic is still the first language, where old traditions live on and where a small population still scratch a living from the often inhospitable land. The influx of summer visitors is an important part of the economy, along with the sale of Aran knitwear.

Of the three islands – Inis Mór (Inishmore), Inis Meáin (Inishmaan) and Inis Oírr (Inisheer) – Inis Mór is the largest, and Kilronan is its main settlement. **Aran's Heritage Centre**, with exhibitions, crafts and an audio-visual show, will steer you towards the many attractions of the islands, from their wonderful beaches to the plentiful historic sites.

There is evidence of prehistoric settlement on the islands. Inis Mór has no less than five stone forts, including the dramatic Dún Aonghasa, perched above a 91m drop to the sea, and Dún Eochla on the island's highest point.

More atmospheric still are the early Christian sites. The islands have a number of ancient churches, including Teampall Bheanáin, which was built in the 6th century, and Teampall Chiaráin, dating from the 8th or 9th centuries.

The islands deserve more than just a day trip, which can only scratch the surface of what they have to offer.

2
Brugh Na Boinne

The valley of the River Boyne east of Slane is a remarkable area containing evidence of Ireland's most ancient history.

This great neolithic cemetery consists of at least 40 burial sites, and the landscape is dotted with standing stones and earthworks, but the crowning glory is the great passage grave at **Newgrange**. Older than Stonehenge, it

Ancient spiral carvings at the tomb entrance

is a mound of enormous dimensions, 11m high and 90m across, with a glittering white quartzite retaining wall encircled with large kerbstones at its base, and these are incised with geometric patterns. Beyond this are the 12 surviving stones of a great circle that originally stretched all the way around the mound.

The entrance to the tomb is marked by a massive stone with triple spiral ornamentations, and above it is an opening through which the rays of the rising sun illuminate the interior of the central chamber for about 15 minutes on just one day of the year – the winter solstice, 21 December (the phenomenon is re-created with artificial light the rest of the year, at the end of the guided tour).

Inside the chamber it is possible to see the intricate construction of the roof, which still keeps out water after about 5,000 years, and the recesses into which the remains of the cremated dead were placed, together with final offerings. There are more of the mysterious geometric patterns on the stones. Much about Newgrange remains a mystery, but there is an interpretive centre at the site which explains what has been discovered.

Try to visit Newgrange outside the peak summer season, when it can get uncomfortably crowded, with lengthy queues for the guided tour, and around the winter solstice, when it is almost impossible to get in. People book years in advance to witness the illumination of the chamber on that morning.

The other major sites of Brugh Na Boinne are the two burial chambers at **Knowth**, northwest of Slane, and the larger but less accessible site at Dowth, to the northeast of the town, which now can only be viewed from the road.

Newgrange and Knowth

31C5

Donore

041-988 0300

Mar–Apr, Oct daily 9:30–5:30; May, late Sep daily 9–6:30; Jun to mid-Sep daily 9–7; Nov–Feb daily 9:30–5; Closed 23–27 Dec. Knowth: Apr–Oct

Coffee shop (€)

Good at visitor centre; poor at monuments

Varies according to site, visitor centre expensive

3
Clonmacnoise

➕ 63C2

✉️ Shannonbridge

☎️ 090-96 74195

🕐 Mid-Mar to mid-May and Sep–Oct daily 10–6; mid-May to Sep daily 9–7; Nov to mid-Mar daily 10:30–5:30

🍴 Coffee shop end Mar–Oct (€)

♿ Access to visitor centre and part of site

✋ Moderate

One of Clonmacnoise's well-preserved round towers

One of the most atmospheric places in Ireland, this ancient monastic city stands in peaceful seclusion beside the River Shannon.

In AD 545 St Ciaran (or Kieran) founded a monastery in this isolated place, cut off from the rest of Ireland by the wide River Shannon and surrounding bogland, and accessible only by boat. In this remote location his monastery grew into an ecclesiastical city, the most important religious foundation of its time in Ireland, and as his burial site it became a place of pilgrimage.

Over the ensuing centuries more and more buildings were added, and the ruins we see today are the most extensive of their kind in the country, including a cathedral, eight churches which were built between the 10th and 13th centuries, two round towers, three high crosses, over 600 early Christian grave slabs, two holy wells and a 13th-century castle. A short way distant is the beautiful Romanesque 'Nun's Church', which was built by Devorgilla, wife of chieftain Tiernan O'Rourke. It was her abduction by Dermot MacMurrough, King of Leinster, that led to conflict which resulted in the Anglo-Norman invasion of Ireland.

Clonmacnoise was also the burial place of the Kings of Connaught and of Tara, including the last High King of Ireland, Rory O'Conor, who was laid to rest here in 1198.

In spite of the remoteness of its setting, Clonmacnoise was known throughout Europe as a centre of excellence in art and literature. Masterpieces of Irish craftsmanship and intricate decoration produced here include the gold and silver Crozier of Clonmacnoise and the Cross of Cong, now in the Treasury of the National Museum in Dublin (➤ 24), and the earliest known manuscript in the vernacular Irish, the *Book of the Dun Cow*, was produced here.

4
The Dingle Peninsula

Of all the glories of the west coast, the Dingle Peninsula is the most beautiful and the most dramatic.

The Dingle Peninsula has many attractions, but best of all is its wonderful coastal scenery. Along the north coast are great sweeping bays, backed by huge brooding mountains; the south has pretty little coves and the lovely Inch beach, and in the west is the incomparable sight of the Blasket Islands off Slea Head. After exploring the coast, the drive across the Connor Pass north from Dingle and over Mount Brandon opens up a whole new perspective, with magnificent views down towards Brandon Bay.

Dingle is the main centre, a delightful town of well-maintained, brightly painted houses and shops with a

✚ 48A2

ℹ Dingle Tourist Office: The Quay (☎ 066-9151188)

🚢 Dingle Bay Eco Tours, The Pier, Dingle (☎ 086-2858802) operate sea tours around Dingle Peninsula, including Blasket Islands (Apr–Oct)

❓ Dingle Way long-distance footpath, (49.6km). Regatta in Aug

picturesque harbour which still supports a working fishing fleet as well as pleasure craft. These include boat trips to see the famous friendly dolphin, Fungi, who lives near the harbour mouth. Dingle has catered for tourists without being swamped by them, and is a lively place with an annual cultural festival and a famous regatta.

Ancient sites on The Dingle include a cliff-top Iron-Age fort near Ventry, Minard Castle, above Dingle Bay, and Gallarus Oratory, a tiny church dating from around the 8th century, between Ballyferriter and Ballynana. Nearby Kilmalkedar Church, dating from the 12th century, contains the Alphabet Stone, inscribed with both Roman and ancient Irish characters.

The Irish style of house painting is beautifully demonstrated in this Dingle street

19

5
The Giant's Causeway

www.ntni.org.uk

75C3 (general area)

172 Ballycastle–
Portrush; summer
services 177 from
Coleraine and 252 from
Belfast and Larne

Portrush (11km)

Causeway Visitor Centre

44 Causeway Road,
Bushmills

028 2073 1855

Daily 10–5 (closes 7
Jul–Aug, 4:30 Nov–Feb)

Tea room (€)

Good

Free. Moderate charge
for car park and extra
charge for audio-visual
theatre

*This unique geological phenomenon,
set on a coastline of outstanding beauty, is one of
the wonders of the natural world.*

About 40,000 columns of basalt cluster on the shoreline here, forming stepping stones from these cliffs down into the water. Most of them are hexagonal, but some have four, five, seven or eight sides, and the tallest rise to around 12m. The only other place in the world where such columns can be seen is on Staffa, an island off the coast of Scotland, and this is simply because they are part of the same formation. Little wonder, then, that the Causeway has been designated a World Heritage Site.

The columns are the result of volcanic action some 60 million years ago, which caused molten basalt to seep up through the chalky bedrock. When it cooled, the rock crystallised into these regular formations, but it would be easy to believe that the blocks were stacked by some giant hand, driven on in its monumental task by the force of some great purpose.

This, of course, is what the ancient Irish believed to be the case, and who else could have completed the task but the legendary giant Finn McCool, the Ulster warrior who was said to inhabit this Antrim headland? When he once

scooped up a clod of earth to throw at a rival, the place he took it from filled with water to become Lough Neagh, the largest lake in the British Isles, and the clod landed in the Irish sea and became the Isle of Man. According to legend, he built the Causeway so that he could cross the sea to reach the lady giant of his dreams, who lived on Staffa – a tall story in more ways than one.

The reality is equally remarkable, but whatever created the Causeway, it is a magnificent sight, particularly when approached on foot from above. There is a cliff-top path all along this stretch of coastline, which can be joined at Blackrock, 2.5km from Causeway Head, or from the **Causeway Visitor Centre**.

The Visitor Centre is on the cliff top, leaving the Causeway in splendid isolation, and is a good introduction to the site. It includes an audio-visual theatre, where a 25-minute show tells the story of the formation of the Causeway. There is also an exhibition area with displays including birdlife and the legend of Finn McCool. A mini-bus runs from here to the Causeway at regular intervals throughout the summer and guided tours are available.

Beside the centre is the **Causeway School Museum**, a reconstructed 1920s schoolroom complete with learning aids and toys of the era.

Causeway School Museum

 52 Causeway Road, Bushmills

028 2073 1777

Jul–Aug daily 11–5

Good

Cheap

Sunlight and shadows emphasise the geometric shapes of the Causeway

6
Kilkenny

🕀 31A2

ℹ️ Shee Alms House, Rose Inn Street (☎ 056-7751500)

🚉 Kilkenny 1.5km

Kilkenny Castle

✉️ The Parade

☎ 056-7721450

🕐 Jun–Sep daily 9:30–7; Apr–May 10:30–5; Oct–Apr 10:30–12:45, 2–5 (guided tours only)

🍴 Tea room May–Sep (€)

♿ Access to ground floor and medieval room

✋ Moderate

Kilkenny Design Centre

✉️ Castle Yard

☎ 056-7722118

🕐 Apr–Dec Mon–Sat 9–6, Sun 10–6; Jan–Mar Mon–Sat 9–6

🍴 Restaurant (€)

Rothe House

✉️ Parliament Street

☎ 056-7722893

🕐 Mar–Nov Mon–Sat 10:30–5; Sun 3–5; Dec–Feb Mon–Sat 1–5, Sun 3–5

♿ Few

✋ Moderate

The richly-coloured walls of Kilkenny Castle's Long Gallery are hung with fine works of art

Narrow medieval streets and alleys linking the great castle and cathedral bear witness to Kilkenny's rich history and architectural heritage.

Standing on a bend of the River Nore, Kilkenny is one of Ireland's most beautiful towns, with delightful little streets to explore, high quality craft studios, good restaurants and an exceptional range of historic buildings.

In medieval times, the town rivalled Dublin in importance and the great **castle** here was the stronghold of the most powerful family in Ireland at the time, the Butlers, Earls and Dukes of Ormonde. Though its origins are back in Norman times, the castle was adapted over the centuries and now reflects the splendour of the 1830s, enhanced by the Butler Gallery of Contemporary Art in the former servants' quarters, the Medieval Room in the South Tower and a multi-purpose cultural facility.

Opposite the castle is the **Kilkenny Design Centre** (► 106), which was established in the 1960s to bring Irish

craftsmanship to new heights of excellence. Not only was the centre resoundingly successful, it became the spearhead of a crafts revival that has attracted fine craft workers from all over the world. **Rothe House**, a Tudor mansion on three sides of a cobbled courtyard, is also worth a visit. Here you'll find a range of restored rooms, the city and county museum and a costume collection.

Kilkenny originally grew up around the 6th-century monastery founded by St Canice, to whom the cathedral is dedicated. Built on the site of the original monastery, it remains one of the finest 13th-century buildings in Ireland and contains impressive monuments of black Kilkenny marble and the Cityscope Exhibition. Beside the cathedral is the well-preserved round tower of the original monastery, which gives wonderful views over the city.

7
Muckross House

Among Ireland's foremost stately homes, Muckross has folk and farm museums and beautiful gardens – all within the Killarney National Park.

When Henry Arthur Herbert, MP for Co Kerry, built his Elizabethan-style mansion in 1843, he could not have found a more perfect site, looking out towards Muckross Lake and surrounded by wonderful scenery that was destined to become a national park. It has elegant rooms, with grand portraits, glittering Venetian mirrors and Chippendale furniture. Maud Bowers Bourne was given the house as a wedding present in 1911. Her family presented the house and estate to the Irish nation in 1932 in her memory.

While the house sums up the lifestyle of the landed gentry in Victorian times, the servants' quarters have been converted into a museum of Kerry folk life, with displays and a weaver's workshop. The new Muckross Craft Centre comprises weaving, pottery and bookbinding workshops. There is also a restaurant and gift shop. Out in the grounds, a 28-hectare farm has been constructed to show farming methods that were used before mechanisation. The rare Kerry cow, a small, black, hardy animal, is being bred here in order to save the herd from extinction.

The gardens at Muckross are renowned for their beauty. Many tender and exotic species thrive in the mild climate, and there are lovely water and rock gardens. A number of nature trails of various lengths begin here, from a one-hour stroll to a 16-km circular Heritage Trail through the most extensive natural yew woods in Europe, which can be walked, cycled (bicycles for hire) or travelled in a horse-drawn jaunting car.

48B2

5km south of Killarney

064-31440

House and gardens: mid-Mar to Oct daily 9–6 (Jul–Aug 9–7); Nov to mid-Mar daily 9–5:30. Farm: Jun–Aug daily 9–6; mid-Mar to May and Sep daily 1–6. Closed winter.

Cafe (€)

From Killarney

Few

House and farm: expensive. House: moderate. Gardens: free

Horse-drawn jaunting cars from Killarney to the house

Beautifully proportioned Muckross House illustrates the lives of the rich landowner and the working artisan

8

The National Museum, Dublin

www.museum.ie

✠ 37C2

✉ Kildare Street, Merrion Street, Benburb Street

☎ 01-6777444

🕐 Tue–Sat 10–5, Sun 2–5

🍴 Cafés at Kildare Street and Collins Barracks (€)

🚌 Cross-city buses

🚆 Pearse station 5-minutes walk; Heuston Station for Collins Barracks

♿ Few; ground floor good

✋ Free

❓ Guided tours depart from the main entrance at regular intervals

Three locations in Dublin house the magnificent and varied collections and priceless treasures of the National Museum.

The oldest of the trio (1857) is the Natural History Museum in Merrion Street, which has one of the finest zoological collections in the world. The ground floor has collections relating to native Irish wildlife, while the upper floor has the World Collection, with many African and Asian species, al overlooked by the skeleton of a 20m whale. Here too is a wonderful collection of glass reproductions of marine specimens.

The Kildare Street branch houses the archaeological collections. The centrepiece is a glittering display of ancient gold – collars, bracelets, dress fasteners, hair ornaments – dating from about 2200 to 700 BC. Some of the gold bears faint traces of Celtic decoration, but the best examples of this are to be found in the National Treasury in the adjacent room. Intricate Celtic patterns are still much in favour, particularly in jewellery, but there is nothing that can compare with the delicate intricacy of the workmanship to be seen here. Some of the patterns, worked in silver and gold many centuries ago, are almost too tiny to be appreciated by the naked eye. There is a huge collection of Viking artefacts, many found during the redevelopment of Wood Quay. The Road to Independence is an evocative exhibition featuring the events and consequences of the Easter Rising and the Civil War.

Across the city, on the north bank of the River Liffey, the restored Collins Barracks house the National Museum's collection of decorative arts, and displays relating to social, political and military history. These include costumes and jewellery, weaponry and furniture, silver, ceramics and glassware, and interactive multimedia terminals provide more interpretation. There is also an interesting section explaining how the museum goes about the process of research, restoration and conservation of its treasures.

The 8th-century Ardagh Chalice represents a triumph of Celtic art and craftsmanship

9
The Rock of Cashel

Ancient seat of the kings of Munster and medieval religious centre, the Rock of Cashel is an awe-inspiring sight.

This single craggy hill, rising out of the surrounding plain and topped by a cluster of wonderful medieval buildings, dominates the skyline. It is a great landmark that draws more than the eye – its romantic outline of ruined towers and graceful arches seems to beckon from a distance.

The great rock was the obvious choice as the fortress of the kings of Munster, who ruled the southern part of Ireland, and Cashel came to prominence in the 4th or 5th century AD. Legend has it that St Patrick came here to baptise the king, and that during the ceremony, the saint accidentally drove the sharp end of his crozier through the king's foot. The king bore the pain unflinchingly because he believed it to be part of the initiation.

🕂 49C2

✉ Rock of Cashel

☎ 062-61437

🕐 Mid-Mar to mid-Jun daily 9:30–5:30; mid-Jun to mid-Sep daily 9–7; mid-Sep to mid-Oct 9–5:30; mid-Oct to mid-Mar daily 9–4:30

🚌 Dublin–Cork buses

♿ Limited access by prior arrangement

✋ Moderate

The dominant building on the rock is the 13th-century St Patrick's Cathedral, roofless now, but still impressive, with its long nave and chancel and a 26m tower. Inside are a wealth of monuments, including important tombs, and the west end is formed by a 15th-century castle, built as the Archbishop's residence.

The Round Tower and Cormac's Chapel are the oldest structures on the Rock, dating from the 11th to 12th centuries, and the chapel contains a remarkable stone sarcophagus carved with sophisticated Celtic patterns.

One of the later buildings, the 15th-century Hall of the Vicars, is one of the first you see on the Rock, with a display of stone carvings in its vaulted undercroft and above it a splendid hall with a minstrels' gallery, huge fireplace and wonderful timbered ceiling.

❓ Guided tours on request. Audio visual, Jun–Sep

Tantalising glimpses of the Rock of Cashel from the approach roads are a stirring sight

25

10
Ulster-American Folk Park

The lives and experiences of Ulster emigrants to the New World are authentically re-created at this splendid open-air museum.

www.folkpark.com

✚ 74B2

✉ 2 Mellon Road, Castletown

☎ 028 8224 3292

🕐 Apr–Sep Mon–Sat 10:30–6, Sun and public hols 11–6:30; Oct–Mar Mon–Fri 10:30–5. Last admission 90 minutes before closing

🍴 Cafe (€)

🚌 273 Belfast– Londonderry

♿ Good

✋ Moderate

❓ Special events to celebrate the Ulster-American connection are held throughout the year. Special celebrations on Independence Day, 4 July

This was the face of a new life in the New World for many Ulster emigrants

In a great tide of emigration during the 18th and 19th centuries, over 2 million people left Ulster for a different life in the New World. Among them was five-year-old Thomas Mellon, who went on to become a judge and founder of the Pittsburg dynasty of bankers, and it is around his childhood home that this museum has been created. Buildings have been reconstructed on the site, giving a complete picture of the world that the emigrants left behind and the one that was awaiting them on the other side of the Atlantic.

The Ulster section includes a typical one-room cottage of the late 18th century, a forge and weaver's cottage, schoolhouse and post office, places of worship and a 19th-century street of shops, with original Victorian shopfronts. Houses include the boyhood homes of John Joseph Hughes, the first Roman Catholic Archbishop of New York, and Robert Campbell, who became a fur trader in the Rockies and a successful merchant in St Louis.

On the dockside, visitors can see a typical merchant's office and a boarding house, where emigrants would await their sailing, then board a reconstruction of the kind of sailing ship which carried them to their new lives.

Beyond this you emerge into the American section of the park, with log houses and barns, including a replica of the six-roomed farmhouse that Thomas Mellon's father built. The buildings contain over 2,000 19th-century artefacts collected in Pennsylvania and Virginia.

What To See

Above: *Garinish Point, Beara Peninsula*
Right: *Kinsale local*

IRELAND

0	40	80	120 km
0	20	40	60 miles

5

Derryvre Mts

Ardara

Donegal

Ballyshannon

Donegal Bay

Erris Head

Sligo

4

▲ 807m

Ballina

Carr on-Sha

Castlebar

Westport

Claremorris

Long

Roscommon

Clifden

Connacht

Tuam

Athlone

3

Connemara

Galway

Ballinasloe

REPUBLI

Galway Bay

Loughrea

OF

Aran Is

Bi

Lough Derg

Ros

Ennis

Nena

Kilrush

IRELAN

Limerick

Thurl

2

Listowel

Tipperary

Tralee

Munster

▲ 918m

Cl

Slea Head

▲ 953m

Mallow

Fermoy

Killarney

Blackwater

▲ 1041m

Caherciveen

Kenmare

Cork

Cobh Y

Macroom

Caba Mts

Kinsale

1

Bantry

Clonakilty

Skibbereen

Mizen Head

A	B	C

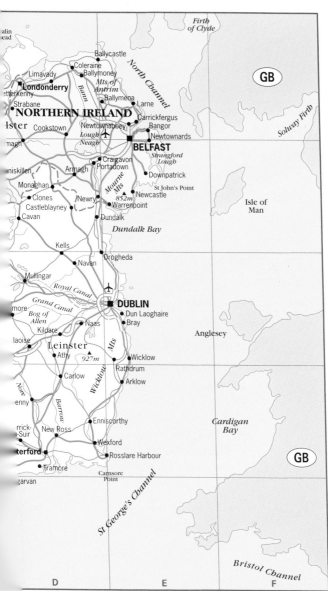

Firth
of Clyde

Ballycastle
Limavady
Coleraine
Ballymoney
Mts of
Antrim
Londonderry
etterkenny
Ballymena
Strabane
Larne
NORTHERN IRELAND
North Channel
GB
ster
Cookstown
Newtownabbey
Carrickfergus
Bangor
Solway Firth
magh
Lough
Neagh
Newtownards
BELFAST
niskillen
Armagh
Craigavon
Portadown
Strangford
Lough
Monaghan
Downpatrick
Clones
Newry
Mourne
Mts
St John's Point
Castleblayney
852m
Newcastle
Cavan
Warrenpoint
Isle of
Man
Kells
Dundalk
Dundalk Bay
Mullingar
Navan
Drogheda
Royal Canal
Grand Canal
more
Bog of
Allen
DUBLIN
Kildare
Naas
Dun Laoghaire
Bray
Anglesey
laoise
Leinster
Mts
Athy
927m
Wicklow
Carlow
Rathdrum
Arklow
Wicklow
Nore
enny
Barrow
Enniscorthy
Cardigan
Bay
rrick-
-Suir
New Ross
terford
Wexford
GB
Rosslare Harbour
Tramore
Carnsore
Point
garvan
St George's Channel
Bristol Channel

D
E
F

The East

The eastern part of Ireland is inevitably dominated by Dublin, a lively city with a lot to see and do, but the east has much more to offer than just the capital. Ireland's most extensive mountain region is just to the south of Dublin in Co Wicklow, where remote, silent valleys and wild exposed mountain tops can be reached in less than half an hour's drive.

Long sandy beaches and golf links stretch along the coast, which remains unspoilt in spite of the presence of the main ferry ports. The resorts retain an old-fashioned appeal.

Inland, the east has some fascinating places to see. To the north of Dublin is a cluster of historic sites including Tara, Kells and Newgrange. Southwest of the capital is the horse-racing centre of Kildare and The Curragh and the wonderful old city of Kilkenny, and in the far south are the pretty villages and fine beaches of the Wexford coast.

> *' Sweet Auburn, loveliest village of the plain, Where health and plenty cheered the labouring swain. '*

OLIVER GOLDSMITH
The Deserted Village (1770)

DUBLIN AND THE EAST

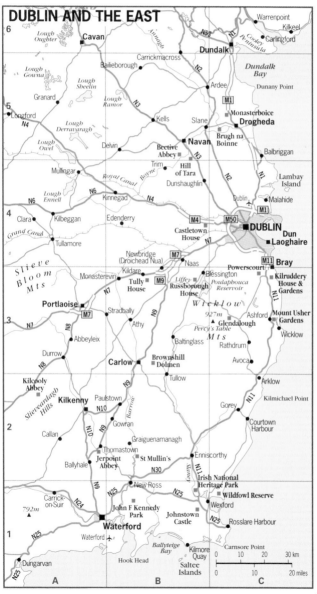

Warrenpoint
Kilkeel
Carlingford
Cooley Peninsula
N53
N1

Cavan
Lough Oughter
6

Ainagh

Dundalk
N2
Dundalk Bay
Dunany Point

Bailieborough
Carrickmacross

Granard
Lough Gowna
Lough Sheelin
Lough Ramor
N3
Ardee
M1
5

Longford
N4
Lough Derravaragh
Lough Owel
Kells
Slane
Monasterboice
Drogheda
Balbriggan

Delvin
Navan
Bective Abbey
Brugh na Boinne
N3

Mullingar
Royal Canal
Boyne
Trim
Hill of Tara
Lambay Island

Lough Ennell
N6
N6
Kinnegad
N4
Dunshaughlin
Dublin
Malahide
N1

Clara
Kilbeggan
Edenderry
Castletown House
M4
M50
M1
DUBLIN
Dun Laoghaire
4

Grand Canal
Tullamore
Newbridge (Droichead Nua)
M7
Naas
N7
Bray
M11

Stieve Bloom Mts
Monasterevin
Kildare
Tully House
M9
Liffey
Blessington
Poulaphouca Reservoir
Powerscourt
Kilruddery House & Gardens
N11

Portlaoise
M7
N7
Russborough House
Wicklow
927m
Glendalough
Ashford
Mount Usher Gardens

N7
N8
Stradbally
N9
Percy's Table
Mts
Wicklow
3

Abbeyleix
Athy
Baltinglass
Rathdrum

Durrow
N8
Carlow
Brownshill Dolmen
Avoca

Kilcooly Abbey
Slieveardagh Hills
Kilkenny
Paulstown
N10
Tullow
Arklow
N11
Kilmichael Point

Callan
N9
N10
Gowran
Barrow
N9
Gorey
Courtown Harbour

Graiguenamanagh
2

Ballyhale
Thomastown
Jerpoint Abbey
St Mullin's
N30
Enniscorthy
Slaney
N11

Carrick-on-Suir
792m
N24
N9
N25
New Ross
N25
Irish National Heritage Park
Wildfowl Reserve
Wexford

John F Kennedy Park
Johnstown Castle
Rosslare Harbour
N25

Waterford
Waterford ✈
Ballyteige Bay
Hook Head
Kilmore Quay
Saltee Islands
Carnsore Point
1

Dungarvan
N25

0   10   20   30 km
0   10   20 miles

A   B   C

Massive medieval walls give no hint of the sumptuous 18th-century interiors of Dublin Castle

Dublin

Part of Dublin's charm is that it only takes a few days of wandering around its attractive streets and leafy squares – and into its atmospheric pubs – to feel that you know the city intimately. And yet, every visit reveals some new delight.

Dublin has everything a capital city should have – magnificent architecture, excellent shopping, lively entertainments and cultural events, superb museums and galleries, colourful parks and gardens and a strong sense of history.

Until now, most of Dublin's attractions have been in the smart areas south of the river. The northside, though not without its shops and a few fine attractions, was a run down area with seedy back streets. Now a multi-million pound redevelopment plan has given it the designer treatment. Wide O'Connell Street has become an attractive, leafy boulevard; behind it in Henry Street the shopping centres have been upgraded and the area now rivals Grafton Street. Smithfield Village is taking shape as an interesting cultural quarter, while the already rejuvenated Temple Bar has continued to grow around Cow's Lane. The docks are being developed and the new LUAS light rail system brings Dubliners in from the suburbs.

What to See in Dublin

DUBLIN CASTLE ✪✪

Soon after the Anglo-Normans arrived in Ireland in the 12th century, King John ordered the building of Dublin Castle and it remained the centre of English power in Ireland until 1922. In spite of its great medieval walls and round bastions, much of the castle is a product of the 18th century, including the splendid State Apartments, where presidents are inaugurated and visiting dignatories received. The Chester Beatty Library, one of the world's best collections of Oriental and European manuscripts, is located in the castle gardens.

DVBLINIA ✪

Developed by the Medieval Trust, Dvblinia tells the story of the city from the arrival of the Anglo-Normans in the 12th century until the closure of the monasteries in 1540. It is housed in a beautifully preserved old building, the former Synod Hall, linked to Christ Church Cathedral by an ancient covered bridge. There is a fine model of medieval Dublin and a collection of artefacts from the National Museum.

✚ 36B3
✉ Dame Street
☎ 01-6777129;
www.dublincastle.ie
◷ Mon–Fri 10–4:45, Sat, Sun, public hols 2–4:45 (state apartments may be closed for functions)
🍴 Self-service restaurant (€)
🚌 Cross-city buses
♿ Good **🚇** Moderate

✚ 36B3
✉ St Michael's Hill
☎ 01-6794611
◷ Apr–Sep daily 10–5; Oct–Mar Mon–Sat 11–4, Sun, public hols 10–4:30
🍴 Tea rooms Jun–Aug (€)
🚌 51b, 78a, 90, 123
♿ Good **🚇** Moderate

DUBLIN WRITERS MUSEUM ✪✪

No other city in the world has spawned so many writers of international repute, including four Nobel prize winners, and this museum is a celebration of that literary heritage. The displays, in the magnificent surroundings of a restored 18th-century mansion, encompass the whole spectrum of Irish works, from the 8th-century *Book of Kells* to the present, taking in Swift, Sheridan, Shaw, Wilde, Yeats, Joyce and Beckett along the way. One room is devoted entirely to children's literature, and there are regular exhibitions and readings.

✚ 36B5
✉ 18/19 Parnell Square North
☎ 01-8722077
🕐 Mon–Sat 10–5 (until 6 Mon–Fri Jun–Aug), Sun & public hols 11–5
🍴 Restaurant (€€) & coffee shop (€)
🚌 10, 11, 11a, 11b, 13, 16a, 19a, 22, 22a, 36
🚉 DART Connolly
♿ None 🚇 Moderate

GUINNESS STOREHOUSE ✪✪✪

Guinness, one of the most potent symbols of Irishness, is now brewed all over the world – at a rate of over 10 million glasses a day – and this is where it all started, founded by Arthur Guinness in 1759. As you enter the Storehouse through a stone arch an escalator whisks you to the heart of the building into what is described as a large glass pint. Within this glass structure you journey through the production process. Entertaining displays and audio-visuals give an insight into the history, manufacture and advertising of Dublin's most famous product. You will end your visit in the rooftop bar, which has excellent views over the city, to sample a free glass of the 'black stuff'.

✚ 36A3
✉ St James's Gate
☎ 01-4044800; www.guinnessstorehouse.com
🕐 Daily 9:30–5, (until 8 Jul–Aug)
🍴 Brewery bar, Gravity bar
🚌 51b, 78a from Aston Quay; 123 from O'Connell Street
♿ Excellent
🚇 Expensive

KILMAINHAM GAOL ✪✪

In its time both a caution and an inspiration, Kilmainham Gaol stands as a monument to the struggle for Irish independence and those leaders of the 1916 Easter Rising who were imprisoned or executed here. It also gives visitors a chillingly realistic impression of what life must have been like for the prisoners who were incarcerated here, be they patriots or petty criminals, from its inauguration in 1796 to 1924.

✚ Off map 36A3
✉ Inchicore Road, Kilmainham
☎ 01-4535984
🕐 Apr–Sep daily 9:30–5; Oct–Mar Mon–Sat 9:30–4, Sun 10–5. Last tour one hour before closing
🚌 51b, 78a, 79
🚇 Moderate

33

🕆 37C2
✉ Merrion Square West
and Clare Street
☎ 01-6615133
🕐 Mon–Sat 9:30–5:30, Thu
9–8:30, Sun 2–5:30
🍴 Restaurant & café (€–€€)
🚌 Cross-city buses
🚆 DART Pearse
♿ Excellent
🎫 Voluntary

🕆 36A4
✉ Smithfield Squre,
Smithfield (from August
2006)
☎ 01-8726340
🕐 Phone for details
🚌 67, 68, 69, 79, 90 (to
Smithfield Square)
♿ Phone for details
🎫 Phone for details

🕆 36A4
✉ Bow Street, Smithfield
Village
☎ 01-817 3838
🕐 Daily 10–5:30, guided
tours only, every 40
minutes
🍴 Restaurant & bar (€–€€)
🚌 67, 67a , 68, 69, 79, 90
♿ Good 🎫 Expensive

🕆 36B4/37C4

NATIONAL GALLERY OF IRELAND 😊😊😊

First opened in 1864, this wonderful gallery has one of the finest collections of European art in the world. Located in the heart of Georgian Dublin, the gallery contains nearly 2,500 paintings, over 5,000 drawings, watercolours and miniatures, over 3,000 prints and more than 300 pieces of sculpture and *objets d'art*. The Millennium Wing, opened in 2002, houses a centre for the study of Irish art and an archive dedicated to the work of Jack B Yeats (1872–1957).

NATIONAL MUSEUM (► 24, TOP TEN)

NATIONAL WAX MUSEUM 😊

This museum brings to life everyone from Irish historical figures to the cult cartoon family the Simpsons. Here you will find life-size re-creations of heroes such as Robert Emmet, Wolfe Tone, Parnell, the leaders of the 1916 rebellion and former presidents. Literary giants are represented with figures of Joyce, Yeats and their contemporaries. You'll find the Chamber of Horrors with accompanying blood-curdling screams, as well as a World of Fairytale and Fantasy. You can see the Popemobile used by Pope John Paul II on his visit to Ireland in 1979 and also the figures of the last four popes. The collection is closed at present, prior to relocating to Smithfield Square in August 2006. Telephone the number given for details.

OLD JAMESON DISTILLERY 😊😊

Explore the history of Irish whiskey-making, which goes back to the 6th century, through exhibits and audio-visual presentations on the site of the old Jameson Distillery in Smithfield Village on the north side of the River Liffey. You can view old and new equipment and watch a working bottling line, then sample a drop of the *uisce beatha*, literally 'water of life'. There is an excellent shop selling a variety of whiskies as well as clothing and posters.

TEMPLE BAR 😊😊😊

Sooner or later, every visitor to Dublin heads for Temple Bar, a lively warren of narrow, cobbled streets just south of the Liffey. There is access from all sides, but the best way in is to walk across the Ha'penny Bridge from the north side of the river and keep straight forward through the arch. You'll find every kind of watering hole and eating place here, from historic pubs like the Oliver St John Gogarty (go for the Sunday brunch music session) to bistros and internet cafés. There are interesting galleries, lively pubs, buskers and music just about everywhere.

TRINITY COLLEGE ✪✪✪

Through the Palladian façade of Trinity College is not only an oasis of peace and quiet in the heart of the busy city centre, but also one of its finest ranges of buildings. The college was founded in 1592 by Elizabeth I, with many fine buildings from the 18th and 19th centuries. The finest of them all is the great **Library**, which contains some of Ireland's greatest treasures. Magnificent illuminated manuscripts on display include the 9th-century *Book of Kells* and the *Book of Armagh*. Also within the college is the **Dublin Experience**, a multimedia show telling the story of Dublin and its people (summer only).

➕ 37C3

Library
- ✉ College Green
- ☎ College: 01-6082320. Library: 01-6081661
- 🕐 All year, Mon–Sat 9:30–5, Sun 12:30–4:30 (from 9:30 Jun–Sep). Closed 10 days at Christmas
- 🚌 Cross-city buses
- ♿ Good
- 🎟 Campus free; libary and Book of Kells expensive

Dublin Experience
- ✉ Trinity College, College Green
- ☎ 01-6081177
- 🕐 Mid-May to late Sep, daily 10–5 (ring for details)
- 🚌 Cross-city buses
- ♿ Good
- 🎟 Moderate

Stacked to its wonderful barrel-vaulted ceiling with ancient volumes, Trinity College Library, is an architectural as well as a literary treasurehouse

35

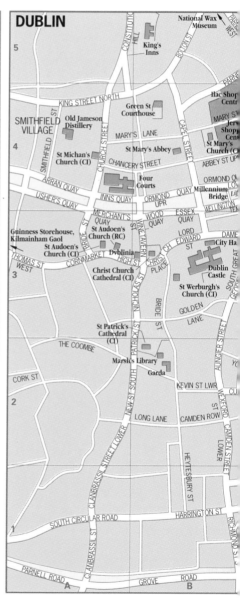

DUBLIN

National Wax Museum

King's Inns

CONSTITUTION HILL

BOTANIC ST

5

KING STREET NORTH

Green St Courthouse

SMITHFIELD VILLAGE

Old Jameson Distillery

SMITHFIELD ST

CHURCH STREET

MARY'S LANE

CAPEL STREET

Hac Shop Centr

MARY ST

Jerv Shop Cen

4

St Michan's Church (CI)

St Mary's Abbey

CHANCERY STREET

St Mary's Church (C

ABBEY ST UP

ARRAN QUAY

Four Courts

ORMOND QU

USHER'S QUAY

INNS QUAY

ORMOND QUAY UPR

Millennium Bridge

LO Lif

WELLINGTON

TEN

Guinness Storehouse, Kilmainham Gaol

MERCHANT'S QUAY

St Audoen's Church (RC)

BRIDE ST

WOOD QUAY

ESSEX QUAY

LORD EDWARD ST

DAME

City Ha

St Audoen's Church (CI)

WINETAVERN ST

Dvblinia

CHRIST CH PLACE

THOMAS ST WEST

CORNMARKET

HIGH ST

Christ Church Cathedral (CI)

NICHOLAS ST

Dublin Castle

SOUTH GREAT

GE

3

St Werburgh's Church (CI)

BRIDE ST

GOLDEN LANE

St Patrick's Cathedral (CI)

THE COOMBE

PATRICK'S ST

AUNGIER STREET

YO

CORK ST

Marsh's Library

Garda

KEVIN ST LWR

CU

NEW ST SOUTH

WEXFORD ST

2

LONG LANE

CAMDEN ROW

CAMDEN STREET LOWER

CLANBRASSIL STREET LOWER

HEYTESBURY ST

HARRINGTON ST

1

SOUTH CIRCULAR ROAD

RICHMOND ST

CLANBRASSIL ST

PARNELL ROAD

GROVE ROAD

A

B

The Bank of Ireland on College Green

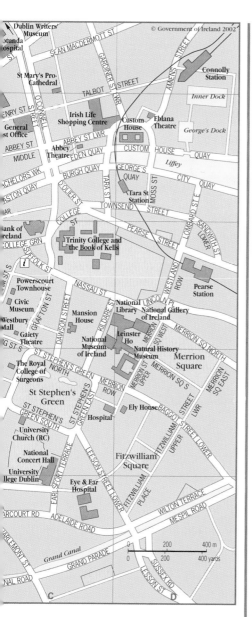

Dublin Writers' Museum

Rotunda Hospital

SEAN MACDERMOTT ST

© Government of Ireland 2002

St Mary's Pro-Cathedral

GARDINER ST

AMIENS STREET

Connolly Station

TALBOT STREET

Inner Dock

HENRY ST

O'CONNELL STREET

Irish Life Shopping Centre

Custom House

Eblana Theatre

George's Dock

General Post Office

ABBEY ST MIDDLE

Abbey Theatre

ABBEY ST LWR

EDEN QUAY

CUSTOM HOUSE QUAY

BACHELORS WK

BURGH QUAY

Liffey

EASTON QUAY

D'OLIER ST

GEORGE'S QUAY

CITY QUAY

TARA ST

Tara St Station

MOSS ST

COLLEGE ST

TOWNSEND STREET

LOMBARD ST E

SANDWITH ST

Bank of Ireland

COLLEGE GRN

Trinity College and the Book of Kells

PEARSE STREET

WESTLAND ROW

Pearse Station

i

SUFFOLK ST

Powerscourt Townhouse

NASSAU ST

National Library

LINCOLN PL

National Gallery of Ireland

Civic Museum

GRAFTON STREET

Mansion House

KILDARE ST

MERRION SQ WEST

MERRION SQ NORTH

Westbury Mall

DAWSON STREET

Leinster Ho

Gaiety Theatre

GRAFTON ST S

National Museum of Ireland

Natural History Museum

Merrion Square

MERRION SQ EAST

The Royal College of Surgeons

ST STEPHEN'S GREEN NORTH

MERRION ROW

MERRION SQ S

St Stephen's Green

ST STEPHEN'S GREEN EAST

Ely House

BAGGOT STREET LWR

ST STEPHEN'S GREEN SOUTH

Hospital

University Church (RC)

LEESON STREET

FITZWILLIAM STREET UPPER

National Concert Hall

EARLSFORT TERRACE

Fitzwilliam Square

University College Dublin

Eye & Ear Hospital

LEESON STREET LOWER

FITZWILLIAM PLACE

WILTON TERRACE

HARCOURT RD

ADELAIDE ROAD

MESPIL ROAD

PARLIAMENT ST

Grand Canal

GRAND PARADE

0   200   400 m
0   200   400 yards

CANAL ROAD

SUSSEX RD

LEESON ST

C

D

Wide O'Connell Street is Dublin's principal thoroughfare north of the River Liffey

A Walk Around Dublin

Distance
About 4km

Time
3–4 hours

Start/end point
Grafton Street
✚ 37C3
🚌 Cross-city buses

Lunch
The Auld Dubliner (€)
✉ 24–25 Temple Bar
☎ 01-6770527

This walk starts in Dublin's most famous shopping street, then takes in many of the city's major attractions.

Walk south along Grafton Street, cross the road and enter the gardens of St Stephen's Green, leaving by the small gate at the left corner. Cross the road and go forward along Kildare Street.

The National Museum, on the right, is Ireland's treasure-house, with some stunning objects and fascinating exhibitions (► 24).

At the end of Kildare Street go left into Nassau Street, then right to College Green with Trinity College on the right (► 35). Follow Westmoreland Street, walk across O'Connell Bridge and turn left alongside the river. Cross Ha'penny Bridge (footbridge), then go through Merchant's Arch into Temple Bar.

This network of little cobbled lanes is worth exploring (► 34).

Turn right into Essex Street East, then take the third left into Eustace Street. At the end turn right along Dame Street.

Dublin Castle is on the left, its medieval origins buried beneath 18th-century recon-structions that house the truly magnificent State Apartments including the Throne Room (► 32).

The picturesque Ha'penny Bridge spans the Liffey near Temple Bar

Keep forward to Christ Church Cathedral.

Begun in the 12th century, beautiful Christ Church is the foremost cathedral in Dublin. Next to it is Dvblinia (► 32).

Go down Fishamble Street to the river. Turn right along the south bank, and at O'Connell Bridge turn right and keep forward back to Grafton Street.

What to See in The East

BRUGH NA BOINNE (► 17, TOP TEN)

CASTLETOWN ✪

Castletown at Celbridge is Ireland's largest and finest Palladian country house, built in the 18th century for William Conolly, Speaker of the Irish House of Commons. The central block, modelled on an Italian *palazzo*, is linked to its two wings by gracefully curving colonnades.

➕ 31B4   ✉ Celbridge
☎ 01-6288252
🛈 Call for opening times
🚌 67 & 67a from Wellington Quay, Dublin
♿ Few   💷 Moderate

The sumptuous interiors, including the Pompeian Gallery, are largely the inspiration of Lady Louisa Lennox, who came to the house on her marriage in 1758. At its heart is a magnificent hall, with sweeping cantilevered staircase and superb plasterwork. Managed by Dúchas, the Irish national Heritage Service.

CEANANNAS MOR (KELLS) ✪

In AD 804 a Columban monastery was founded at Kells by monks who had fled the Viking raids on Iona. It was to become one of the great centres of Celtic Christianity, and it was here that the magnificently decorated version of the Gospels, the *Book of Kells*, was completed. This is now a prized possession of Dublin's Trinity College Library (► 35) after being moved there during the Cromwellian wars, but replicas are on display in Kell's Heritage Centre, along with a multi-media exhibition that entices you to explore the various sites throughout Kells.

➕ 31B5
✉ Kells Heritage Centre, The Courthouse, Headfort Place
☎ 046-9247840
🛈 May–Sep Mon–Sat 10–5:30, Sun and public hols 2–6; Oct–Apr Tue–Sat 10–5
♿ Good
💷 Moderate

The town's street pattern still reflects the circular shape of the monastery, from which only a round tower and the tiny St Columcille's House remain. The original doorway of the house was 2.4m above ground level, a defensive measure which reflected troubled times. Close to the round tower, in the churchyard are three elaborately carved stone crosses, also from the 9th century. A fourth, with 30 decorative panels, stands in Market Square, but its shaft was damaged by its one-time use as a gallows.

Intricate plasterwork at Castletown

GLENDALOUGH ✪✪✪

Deep in the heart of the Wicklow Mountains (➤ 45) are the atmospheric remains of a remarkable monastic city which was founded in the 6th century by St Kevin and remained an important place of pilgrimage well into the 18th century.

Many legends surround the mysterious St Kevin. He is said to have come to Glendalough to avoid the advances of a beautiful redheaded woman with 'unholy eyes', and that he rolled himself, and his putative lover, in stinging nettles to dampen their desire. He may also have hurled the lady into an icy lake to cool her ardour.

Some of the remains, accessible only by boat, are on the south side of the Upper Lake and include the reconstructed Templenaskellig and St Kevin's Bed, a small cave reached after a difficult climb.

The settlement developed mainly between the 10th and 12th centuries, when most of the buildings were erected. These include St Kevin's Church, an oratory known as St Kevin's Kitchen, the fine 30m round tower and the Cathedral of St Peter and St Paul. There are several other churches and monastic buildings around the site, as well as numerous gravestones and crosses, including the plain granite St Kevin's Cross, standing 3.5m high. The **Visitor Centre** by the first car park displays many antiquities found in the valley and is the starting point of guided tours.

An atmosphere of peace and seclusion still surrounds the monastic remains at Glendalough

➕ 31C3

Glendalough Visitor Centre
☎ 040-445325/445352
🕐 Mid-Mar to mid-Oct daily 9:30–6; mid-Oct to mid-Mar daily 9:30–5
🚌 Can be reached on coach tours from Dublin (Bus Éireann)
♿ Poor; good to visitor centre 💷 Cheap

➕ 31B1
✉ Ferrycarrig
☎ 053-20733
🕐 Mar–Oct daily 9:30–6:30 (5:30 Nov–Feb). Last admission 3
🍴 Restaurant (€€)
♿ Good
💷 Moderate

IRISH NATIONAL HERITAGE PARK ✪✪

On the River Slaney, a little way west of Wexford, is the Irish National Heritage Park, which re-creates Irish life over a period of about 9,000 years, ending with the Anglo-Norman period. No fewer than 14 historical sites have been re-created amidst the maturing woodland of the 14-hectare site. The trappings and paraphernalia of everyday life through the ages helps to bring it all to life, and the park successfully combines the requirements of tourism with serious historical content.

JERPOINT ABBEY 😊😊

Jerpoint Abbey is one of Ireland's finest monastic ruins. The first religious house here was a Benedictine abbey, founded around 1158, but by 1180 it had been taken over by the Cistercians. Substantial remains of buildings from the 12th to the 15th centuries tower impressively above the main road. For all its size and presence, however, what is most interesting here are the amusing carvings along the restored cloister arcade, the fine monuments and various effigies.

➕ 31A2
✉ Thomastown
☎ 056-7724623
🕐 Jun to mid-Sep 9:30–6; mid-Sep to Oct 10–5; mid-Mar to May 10–4
♿ Good to visitor centre
💰 Cheap

KILDARE 😊😊

This fine old county town has an attractive central square and some medieval buildings. St Brigid's Cathedral is on the site of a monastery founded in AD 490 and near by is a 10th-century round tower with wonderful views. The other tower in the town is that of the 15th-century castle.

Kildare is at the heart of horse-racing country, and Irish-bred horses are among the most prized in the world. The **National Stud** at Tully House gives visitors an insight into the development and control of these magnificent animals.

The **Japanese Gardens** at Tully House, landscaped in 1906 to 1910 by the Japanese gardener Tasa Eida, include a tea house and a miniature village carved from rock from Mount Fuji. The gardens symbolise the life of man, taking the pilgrim-soul on a journey from Birth to Eternity.

St Fiachra's Garden seeks to re-create the landscape of rocks and water that inspired spirituality in early monastic life. At its heart is a superb bronze statue of St Fiachra, noted for his love of nature, sitting contemplatively, holding up a seed. A stone hermitage contains pieces of sparkling Waterford Crystal representing rocks and flowers.

➕ 31B3

National Stud/Japanese Gardens/St Fiachra's Gardens
✉ Tully, Kildare
☎ 045-521617
🕐 Mid-Feb to mid-Nov daily 9:30–6
🍴 Restaurant (€€)
🚌 Dublin–Kildare (bus stops at gate)
♿ Good to stud and St Fiachra; poor to Japanese Garden 💰 Expensive

Horses at the renowned National Stud, Kildare

Did you know ?

Colonel William Hall-Walker, later Lord Wavertree, established the National Stud and the Japanese Gardens. He housed his racehorses in 'lantern' boxes with skylights so that the moon and stars could influence his thorough breeding programme. He would reject any foal born with an unfavourable astrological chart, and was surprisingly successful.

KILKENNY (▶ 22, TOP TEN)

31C4

Malahide Castle
☎ 01-8462184
🕐 Apr–Sep Mon–Sat 10–5,
Sun & public hols 10–6;
Oct–Mar Mon–Sat 10–5,
Sun & public hols 11–5
🍴 Restaurant (€€)
🚌 42 from Dublin
🚆 DART Malahide
👋 Moderate

31C5
✉ Collon
🕐 Always accessible
🍴 Forge Gallery Restaurant
(€€–€€€), Collon
☎ 041-982 6267

31C3
✉ Enniskerry
☎ 01-2046000
🕐 Daily 9:30–5:30 (dusk in
winter)
🍴 Restaurant and café
(€–€€); kiosk at waterfall
🚆 DART to Bray, then bus
185 to Enniskerry
♿ Good
👋 Expensive

MALAHIDE ✪✪

The town of Malahide is a traditional seaside resort that
has also become a popular residential area for commuters
to Dublin. One of its great attractions is that it is particularly
well endowed with good restaurants, but its main boast is
the magnificent **castle**. It is one of Ireland's oldest, with a
romantic medieval outline that has changed little in its 800
years, but the interior has been transformed over the
centuries, and now contains superb Irish furniture and
paintings, including a historic portrait collection which is, in
effect, a National Portrait Gallery.

MONASTERBOICE ✪✪

One of Ireland's best-known Christian sites,
Monasterboice was founded by St Buite in the 6th century
and thrived for 600 years, until the new Cistercian
Mellifont Abbey superceded it in importance. The site
includes a remarkable 10th-century round tower which
stands 33m high (without its roof) and offers a good view
of the encircling ramparts. There are also three superb high
crosses, of which the South Cross (Muiredach's) is the
best, a 6m monolith with distinctive sculptural detail of
biblical scenes. The West Cross is the tallest, and has
some expressive carving, but has suffered from erosion.
The North Cross has a plain, modern shaft.

POWERSCOURT HOUSE AND GARDENS ✪✪✪

Amid the wild landscape of the Wicklow Mountains
(➤ 43) is one of the most superb gardens in Europe.
Powerscourt Gardens were originally laid out in the mid-
17th century to complement the magnificent Powerscourt
House. Great formal terraces step down the south-facing
slope, with distinctive mosaics of pebbles (taken from the
beach at Bray). There are beautiful lakes and fountains,
statues and decorative ironwork, American, Italian and
Japanese gardens and, in contrast, charming kitchen

*The formal gardens at
Powerscourt are
considered to be among
the finest in Europe*

gardens and a little pet's cemetery. Keen gardeners who are inspired by all the beauty can visit the Pavilion garden centre and take a little piece of it home.

In every direction is a backdrop of mountain peaks and Ireland's highest waterfall plunges 121m into a picturesque valley within the park. The Glen of the Dargle is a wooded gorge, dotted with modern sculpture. More than 20 years after it was destroyed by fire, Powerscourt House reopened its doors. It houses an exhibition about its history, which includes a visit to the former ballroom, an excellent gallery of shops and a terrace café.

The loveliest 'power station' in Ireland, the Poulaphouca Reservoir is part of the River Liffey hydroelectric scheme

THE WICKLOW MOUNTAINS ✪✪

Just a short distance from the centre of Dublin is this wonderfully secluded area of high mountains and peaceful valleys (➤ 45). Lugnaquilla is the highest point, at 943m, and is the source of the River Slaney. Two scenic passes cross the mountains from east to west – the Sally Gap on the old Military Road and the Wicklow Gap further south.

Great forests clothe many of the mountain slopes, including Coollatin Park near Shillelagh, in the south, which preserves remnants of the oak forests which are said to have supplied the roof timbers for Dublin's St Patrick's Cathedral and London's Palace of Westminster. Near Blessington is the great Poulaphouca Reservoir, providing Dublin with both water and electricity, with scenic lakeside drives and waterbus cruises.

Signs of historic habitation include ancient hillforts and stone circles, the monastic site at Glendalough (➤ 40) and the mansions of Powerscourt at Eniskerry (➤ above) and Russborough House, near Blessington. More sinister associations are attached to the creepy ruin of the Hell Fire Club on top of Mount Pelier near Tallaght. Ask the locals to tell you its story, then climb up (in daylight!) for a look. The views are wonderful.

31C3

Johnnie Fox's, Glencullen

01-2955647

✚ 31B1

Wexford Wildfowl Reserve
✚ 31C1
✉ North Slob
☎ 053-23129
🕐 Easter–Sep daily 9–6;
Oct–Mar daily 10–5
🚌 No public transport to the reserve
♿ Good to one hide
🎫 Free

The attractive main street in historic Wexford

WEXFORD

With its huge natural harbour and its location close to the southeastern point of Ireland, over the centuries Wexford was the natural landing place for travellers from Wales, Cornwall and France. The Vikings were the first settlers in the 9th or 10th century, and the town's network of narrow lanes that cluster behind the waterfront are a legacy of those far-off times. Wexford was also the first Irish settlement to fall to the invading Anglo-Normans in 1169, and soon afterwards, at Selskar Abbey, the Anglo-Irish treaty was signed.

Wexford is an interesting mixture of working county town, with busy streets, lively pubs and a famous opera festival, and historic Heritage Town, with some of its 14th-century town wall still intact. After its award-winning restoration, the four-storey West Gate now houses the Heritage Centre, with an audio-visual presentation about the town.

The nearby mudflats known as The Slobs are now the **Wexford Wildfowl Reserve**, with a research station, a visitor centre, hides and a lookout tower. The reserve is of international importance, having one-third of the world's population of Greenland White-fronted geese.

About 6.5km southwest of the town is Johnstown Castle, home of the **Irish Agricultural Museum**, housed in historic estate farm buildings. It has a wide range of agricultural displays and replicas of a forge and other workshops.

Irish Agricultural Museum
✉ Johnstown Castle
☎ 053-42888
🕐 Jun–Aug Mon–Fri 9–5, Sat, Sun & public hols 11–5; Mar–May Sep–Nov, Mon–Fri 9–12:30, 1:30–5, Sat, Sun & public hols 2–5
🍴 Coffee shop, Jul–Aug (€)
♿ Few
🎫 Moderate

Did you know ?

In the area of Bridgetown, to the south of Wexford, a distinct dialect exists. The people here use the oldest Anglo-Norman speech in Ireland because the original Anglo-Norman colonists who arrived in the 12th century intermarried among themselves and were never assimilated by the native Irish.

A Tour of the Wicklow Mountains

This drive includes the beautiful Wicklow Mountains, two of Ireland's finest gardens and the monastic remains at Glendalough.

Leave Wicklow on the Dublin road and continue to Ashford.

Mount Usher Gardens, off to the right along the banks of the River Vartry, are a superb example of 'wild gardens'.

In Ashford turn left, then fork right, following signs for 'Roundwood'. At the T-junction by Roundwood church, turn left, then fork right, signposted 'Enniskerry'. Continue, following signs for Enniskerry.

The entrance to Powerscourt House and Gardens is on a bend at the beginning of the village. The gardens here are among the finest in Europe, and Powerscourt Waterfall is Ireland's highest.

In Enniskerry, turn left, and after 8km reach Glencree. At the next junction head for 'Sally Gap, Glendalough'. After another 8km turn right, and keep following signs for 'Blessington' until reaching the N81. Turn left. After 3km turn left on to the R758 signposted 'Valleymount, Lake Drive'. Continue, following signs for Glendalough.

This ancient settlement is one of Ireland's major attractions, with atmospheric ruins.

Return to the junction and go forward through Laragh. After 5km turn right, signposted 'Arklow, Rathdrum R755'. In Rathdrum follow signs for 'Avoca'. At T-junction, turn left, then bear right, signposted 'Dublin'. After 13km turn right to return to Wicklow.

Distance
117km

Time
About 5–6 hours, depending on attractions visited

Start/end point
Wicklow
✚ 31C3

Lunch
Powerscourt Terrace Café (€)
✉ Powerscourt House
☎ 01-204 6070

Powerscourt Waterfall, plunging 122m into the valley, is spectacular after heavy rain

The South

A great many visitors to Ireland head straight for this southwestern corner and ignore the rest of the country completely – which is a shame, but is entirely understandable. Here you will find the great fjord-like bays which cut into the rocky west coast, between the magnificent peninsulas of The Dingle, the Iveragh (better known as The Ring of Kerry), the Beara and the smaller, but no less beautiful Sheep's Head and Mizen peninsulas.

The south coast is less spectacular, but has some wonderful beaches, fine resorts and charming fishing villages such as Kinsale. Aim to be hungry when you visit here – the village is known as the Gourmet Capital of Ireland.

The southwest is not all coast and scenery. Ireland's second city, Cork, and its third, Limerick, are in this area, while towards the east are the historic city of Waterford, the great Rock of Cashel and the ancient towns and castles along the River Suir.

> *'Tis the bells of Shandon*
> *That sound so grand on*
> *The pleasant waters*
> *of the River Lee.'*

FATHER FRANCIS O'MAHONY
(FATHER PROUT)
The Bells of Shandon (c1830s)

The tranquil setting for St Finbarr's Chapel, Gougane Barra, West Cork

Cork

Cork is the Republic's second largest city. At its heart is the wide St Patrick's Street, with lots of little lanes leading off that are a delight to explore. Cork is a proud, friendly city, where tradition and modern life blend easily together. It has a vibrant arts and cultural scene and was designated the European Capital of Culture for 2005.

The name Cork comes from the Irish word 'Corcaigh' meaning marsh. The older part of the city is on an island in the River Lee. From this island a network of streets branch out, giving a blend of broad malls and narrow lanes, spires, Georgian houses, busy markets and bridges that make up Cork's most prelevant features. The Lee flows into the deep waters of Cork Harbour, and this harbour brought much of the city's prosperity over the centuries. It also brought the Vikings in AD 820 and later the Anglo-Normans. Cork suffered at the hands of William of Orange in 1690 and by the 'Black and Tans' in the 20th century. Cork has had its challenges over the centuries but has risen to them all and remains a city of unique character.

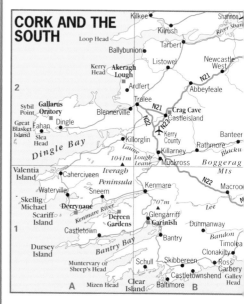

The graceful spires of St Finbarr's Cathedral tower over the stately waters of the River Lee

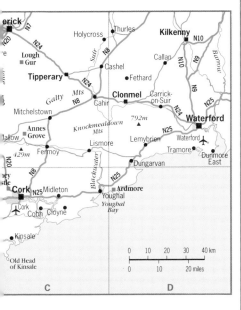

What to See in Cork

CORK BUTTER MUSEUM

Butter is undoubtedly an odd subject for a museum, until you discover that Shandon's Butter Exchange was the largest butter market in the world, attracting customers from distant continents, and that its brand was internationally recognised as a symbol of top quality. It really is worth a visit.

CORK CITY GAOL

The thought of going to prison, if only for the afternoon, may not have an immediate appeal, but Cork's former gaol is now a museum that re-creates prison life in the 19th century in an entertaining way, and also presents a good social history of the city. The former Governor's House houses the Radio Museum Experience, incorporating a 1927 studio and the RTE Museum Collection.

CORK PUBLIC MUSEUM

Few city museums have such a lovely setting as this. There are 7.5 hectares of beautiful parkland surrounding the Georgian House which displays a wide range of collections illustrating the economic and social history of Cork, along with its Civic Regalia.

CRAWFORD ART GALLERY

Already one of Ireland's finest art galleries, the Crawford now has a wonderful new extension. Above a new glass frontage on Half Moon Street, the gallery wall swoops out over the pavement like the hull of a ship, to reflect Cork's maritime heritage. The theme continues inside, in the three curving ceiling sections above the new upper galleries that are flooded with natural light. The lower gallery has a more restrained environment. The next phase of the Crawford Development Plan is to improve the historic original building and the grounds. As well as its permanent collection of works by Irish artists, the gallery has a lively programme of temporary exhibitions.

ST ANNE'S CHURCH

The tall square tower of St Anne's church, capped by a gilded weather vane in the shape of a salmon, is Cork's best-known landmark. The tower is faced in red and white sandstone – the colours of Cork. Built in 1722, St Anne's is the oldest parish church still in continuous use in Cork. Its famous bells, which visitors can ring, chime each quarter hour. Sunday services are at 9AM and 10:15AM.

49C1
O'Connell Square, Shandon
021-4300600; www.corkbutter.museum
Mar–Oct daily 10–1, 2–5
3 from city centre
Good Cheap

49C1
Sunday's Well
021-4305022
Mar–Oct daily 9:30–5; Nov–Feb daily 10–4
Coffee shop (€)
Mostly good
Moderate

49C1
Fitzgerald Park, Mardyke
021-4270679
Mon–Fri 11–1, 2:15–5 (until 6 Jun–Aug); Sat 11–1, 2:15–4; Apr–Sep Sun 3–5   Free

---

49C1
Emmet Place
021-4273377
Mon–Sat 10–5. Closed 25 Dec–1 Jan, Sun & public hols
Crawford Gallery Restaurant (€€)
All city buses
Cork (10-minute walk)
Good
Free

49C1
Church Street, Shandon
021-4505906
Apr–Sep 9–6; Oct–Mar 10–4
3 from city centre
None Moderate

A Walk Around Cork

This walk takes in the main shopping street and the art gallery, before crossing the River Lee to Shandon, then on to the Cork Public Museum in Fitzgerald Park.

Walk along Grand Parade away from the statue, then bear right into St Patrick Street. At the pedestrian crossing, turn left and go along Academy Street to the Crawford Art Gallery (➤ 50).

This fine municipal gallery has a particularly good collection of local landscapes.

Continue round the corner and cross the bridge. Turn left, then bear right following signs to Shandon for the Butter Museum (➤ 50). Just off the square is St Anne's Church (➤ 50).

Now unused, this former church is one of Cork's great landmarks, with its lofty tower and famous bells.

Continue, passing the Shandon Arms on the left, and at the end go forward along Chapel Street.

Opposite the end of Chapel Street is the Cathedral of St Mary and St Ann, with a beautiful, bright interior and some interesting monuments.

Turn left along Cathedral Street, then left down Shandon Street to the river. Turn right to walk along the nearside riverbank, then at the end cross a footbridge. Follow the riverside wall then go forward between Mercy Hospital and Lee Maltings. At the end turn right and walk along Dyke Parade until you reach the gates to Fitzgerald Park on the right. The Cork Public Museum is just inside the gates (➤ 50).

A view of St Finbarr's Cathedral and South Gate Bridge

Distance
About 2.5km

Time
About 3 hours

Start point
Grand Parade
🚌 All city centre buses

End point
Fitzgerald Park
🚌 8 to city centre

Lunch
Bells Bar and Bistro (€–€€)
✉ Quality Shandon Court Hotel, Shandon
☎ 021-4551793
♿ Good

What to See in The South

BANTRY

This lovely little town, at the head of the beautiful Bantry Bay, is a busy fishing port, its harbour overlooked by a statue of that intrepid Irish seafarer, St Brendan. Close by is the entrance to **Bantry House**, an exquisite Georgian mansion. The elegant interior contains a fine collection of furniture, Pompeiian mosaics and tapestries. The beautiful Italianate gardens have a wonderful view over the bay and delicate plants thrive in the mild climate.

THE BEARA PENINSULA

Less well known than the Ring of Kerry and The Dingle, The Beara Peninsula is just as beautiful, with its rocky, indented coastline and offshore islands. The Caha Mountains and the Slieve Miskish Mountains form its spine, creating a dramatic inland landscape, and the Healy Pass, which zig-zags across the Caha range, has wonderful views (▶ 59).

The **Sub-Tropical Gardens** on Garinish Island, in a sheltered inlet of Bantry Bay, reached by ferry from Glengarriff, is the Beara's main attraction. It is a magnificent Italian garden, with a world-famous collection of plants, which thrive here because of the warming effect of the Gulf Stream.

BLARNEY CASTLE

The 'gift of the Blarney' is known all over the world and this is where you get it. By leaning backwards over a sheer drop (protected by railings) from the castle battlements and kissing a particular piece of rock, any visitor can go home endowed with a new eloquence. The Blarney Stone is reached by ancient stone spiral staircases through the ruins of the 15th-century castle, which would be well worth a visit even without its notoriety. The castle is set in lovely grounds, and is one of Ireland's most visited places.

48B1

Bantry House
- 027-50047
- Mar–Oct daily 9–6
- Coffee shop (€)
- Cork–Bantry bus
- Few
- Expensive

48A1

Sub-Tropical Gardens
- Garinish Island, off Glengarriff
- 027-63040
- Jul–Aug Mon–Sat 9:30–6:30, Sun 11–6:30; Apr–Jun, Sep Mon–Sat 10–6:30, Sun 11–6:30; Mar, Oct Mon–Sat 10–4:30, Sun 1–5
- Glengarriff main street; Kenmare–Bantry bus passes through Glengarriff
- Glengarriff main street
- Few
- Moderate (separate charge for ferry)

The gift of eloquence is not given away lightly at Blarney Castle

49C1
- Blarney, Co Cork
- 021-4385210; www.blarneycastle.ie
- Jun–Aug daily 9–7; May and Sep 9–6:30; 9–dusk rest of year
- Few Expensive

KENMARE ✪✪

Situated at the head of Kenmare Bay and surrounded by majestic mountains, earns Kenmanre its Irish name 'Neidin' or little nest. Ireland's first planned town was designed by William Petty in 1670. Today, traditional pubs, craft shops and art galleries combine well with first-class hotels, guesthouses and award-winning restaurants. The Heritage Centre explains the history of Kenmare using personal audio tours and exhibitions include exhibits on Kenmare lace and the Nun of Kenmare.

CASHEL ✪✪✪

The town tends to be overshadowed by the great Rock of Cashel (▶ 25) which dominates the skyline, but as one of Ireland's Heritage Towns, it is well worth a visit in its own right. A good place to start is City Hall, which has historical and folklore displays relating to the town. There is also a **Folk Village**, with a series of 18th- to 20th-century house fronts, shops and memorabilia, and the **Brù Borù Heritage Centre**, which offers a cultural experience through its folk theatre, evening banquets, exhibitions and traditional music sessions. Added in 2001, 'The Sounds of History' exhibition is located in a subterranean setting where Ireland's musical heritage is reactivated and enhanced.

✚ 49B1
ℹ Tourist Information
  (☎ 064-41233)
🍴 P F McCarthy's, Main
  Street (€€)

✚ 49C2
🚌 Dublin–Cork buses
🚉 Thurles 18km
♿ Good

Folk Village
✉ Dominic Street
☎ 062-62525
🕐 Daily 9:30–7:30 (closes 6
  in winter)
♿ Good
✋ Moderate

Brù Borù Heritage Centre
☎ 062-61122
🕐 Mid-Jun to mid-Sep daily
  9–11PM, shows Tue–Sat
  9PM; mid-Sep to mid-Jun,
  Mon–Fri 9–1, 2–5, no
  shows
🍴 Self-service restaurant
  (€). Combined evening
  meal and show (€€)
♿ Good
✋ Exhibition moderate;
  show expensive

*Beautiful Bantry Bay
offers good fishing, and
has a mussel farm too*

53

➕ 48A2

ℹ Killarny Tourist
Information (☎ 064-
31633)

🍴 Blind Piper Bar
Restaurant (€–€€),
Caherdaniel (☎ 066-
9475126)

THE DINGLE (▶ 19, TOP TEN)

THE RING OF KERRY ✪✪✪

The road which encircles the Iveragh peninsula is popularly
known as the Ring of Kerry, an exceptionally scenic circular
route of 107km if you start and finish in Killarney. From
here you go south through the national park to Kenmare,
then strike out along the north shore of the Kenmare
estuary, through the lovely resort of Parknasilla. The
famous Great Southern Hotel here has played host to the
rich and famous for many years.

Farther along is Caherdaniel. The route heads north
from here around Ballinskelligs Bay to Waterville, then on
to Cahersiveen, the 'capital' of the peninsula and birthplace
of Daniel O'Connell. It also has an interesting Heritage
Centre. The road then heads eastwards, with Dingle Bay
to the north, through Killorglin, a market town famous for
its Puck Fair in August, then back to Killarney.

As if the wonderful coast and mountain scenery was
not enough, the peninsula is also blessed with a warm
Gulf Stream climate.

*The nearest thing to
commuters ever seen on
the west Kerry coast*

KILLARNEY ✪✪

Killarney is one of the busiest tourist towns in Ireland, not for its own attractions so much as for its surroundings. There are lots of interesting shops, pubs and restaurants here, but Killarney is essentially a base for exploring the beauties of Kerry, and is the traditional starting point for the Ring of Kerry. The Killarney National Park, 10,000 hectares of beautiful mountains, woodland and lakes, is right on the doorstep, and is the setting for Muckross House (► 23).

➕ 48B2

> ### Did you know ?
>
> *Jarveys are the drivers of the horse-drawn jaunting cars you will see lined up along the roadside in Killarney. Haggling over the fee is an acceptable part of the deal, but remember that you are not just paying to get from A to B – Jarveys are an intrinsic part of the Killarney experience and will usually spin a yarn or two along the way.*

KINSALE ✪✪✪

Kinsale is a delightful little town 29km from Cork City. It offers visitors such things as sailing, scenery, history and good food. The annual Gourmet Festival in October and a Good Food Circle work to maintain the town's famously high culinary standards. Historically, Kinsale is remembered for the 1601 battle, when a Spanish fleet came to aid Hugh O'Neill's struggle against the English. The Irish/Spanish force were defeated, thus marking the decline of the old Gaelic order, with the 'Flight of the Earls' to Europe. The late 17th-century Charles Fort at Summercove is open to visitors, while James Fort is in ruins but is still worth a visit for the grand views of the town and harbour. It was off this coast that the *Lusitania* was sunk by a German submarine in 1915, with the losss of 1,500 lives. Places of interest to visit in Kinsale are the Courthouse, c1600, which now houses a regional museum and also the 12th-century church of St Multose.

➕ 49C1
ℹ Tourist Information (☎ 021-4772234)
🍴 Fishy Fishy (€–€€), Guardwell (☎ 021-4774453)

Imaginative paintwork on this Kinsale exterior reflects the village's close connection with both the sea and seafood

Food & Drink

Eating out in Ireland is as unhurried an experience as anything else in this relaxing island, and the generally high standard of cooking and service, and the quality of the ingredients, is certainly well worth savouring.

In all the major towns and cities there is a good variety of food on offer, and traditional Irish cuisine has enjoyed a revival, often with the occasional international influence.

Away from the fast-food places, eating out in Ireland is not particularly cheap, but travellers on a budget will find a choice of restaurants throughout the country which offer a 'tourist menu' of good food at reasonable prices.

Specialities to look out for include local cheeses, of which there are many, such as the delicious Cashel Blue, Cooleeney, St Killian, Durrus, Chetwynd Blue and Mizen. Irish seafood is also legendary, with fresh lobster, oysters, mussels and scallops.

Above: *oysters and Guinness – food of the gods – are widely available around the coast from September to April*
Top right: *one of many varieties of homemade local bread cakes*

'Bog Butter'
In the days long before refrigerators, butter was stored in wooden barrels, buried in the peat bogs. Not only did it stay fresh for a long time, it was safe from butter burglars. 'Bog Butter' is still unearthed occasionally during peat cutting.

Irish Cuisine

Irish cooking has a reputation for being plain but plentiful, which does it something of a disservice, because the traditional dishes have wonderfully rich flavours and interesting taste combinations.

In recent years dishes that were designed to satisfy the hunger of hard-working farmers and fishermen have been adapted to suit the lesser appetites of those who have done no more than a bit of gentle sightseeing. What was once dismissed as 'peasant food' has now become a delicacy, such as *drisheen* (black pudding), *cruibeens* (pigs' trotters), Dublin coddle (a sausage stew), beef stewed in Guinness and, of course, Irish stew. Potato dishes such as Champ (mashed with chives and butter) or Colcannon (mashed, mixed with leek, butter, cabbage, cream and nutmeg) are a tasty accompaniment, and adventurous diners can sample edible seaweed in the form of dulce or carrageen pudding.

Irish bread is not just something to make a sandwich with. There are lots of tasty varieties that only need a spreading of butter or a side dish of home-made soup. Soda bread, or wheaten bread, made with stone-ground flour, has a wonderful flavour and texture and there are lots of fruity tea breads such as Barm brack. There is even a potato bread (mashed potato mixed with flour and egg) that is cooked on a griddle and often served with the enormous traditional Irish breakfast of bacon, eggs, sausage and black (or white) pudding.

Whiskey and Beer

Think of Irish beer and it is probably a pint of Guinness that springs to mind. Sold in at least 30 countries world wide, Guinness is a great symbol of Irishness, but undoubtedly tastes best on Irish soil, with its cool, biting taste and thick creamy head. Hard on the heels of Guinness are two other stouts, Beamish and Murphy's, both brewed in Cork, while Smithwicks offers a smooth-tasting bitter which is similar to English beer. Lager is also widely available to those who prefer a more continental taste.

Irish whiskey also has a world market and has a wonderful clean flavour, quite different from Scotch whisky or American bourbon. Four main brands are produced by the Irish Distillers company – Bushmills, Jameson, Powers and Paddy, with pure malts of various ages as well as blended whiskey. The Bushmills Distillery in Northern Ireland and Jameson's at Midleton, Co Cork give guided tours which explain the distilling process.

Breweries and Distilleries

At one time Cork had 10 distilleries and 30 breweries. Now there are just two breweries – Beamish and Murphy's – and an Irish Distillers' plant. This company, a subsidiary of the French Ricard (Pernod) company, actually produces all of the Irish whiskey brands. Just east of the city, at Midleton, the Jameson Heritage Centre tells the history of Irish whiskey.

The instantly recognisable labels of some of Ireland's famous whiskeys

LIMERICK ⭐⭐

The Republic's third largest city, Limerick is an attractive, prosperous and lively place with a long and distinguished history. It is also a cultural centre, well endowed with theatres, art galleries and museums – notably the **Hunt Museum**. Located in the elegant 18th-century Custom House, the gallery has one of the greatest private collections of art and antiquities in the country.

The wide River Shannon flows through the city, overlooked by the massive **King John's Castle** and crossed by many fine bridges. The oldest part of the city is on King's Island, first settled by the Vikings, and it is here that the most important historical sites are found, including the castle and the 12th-century Protestant cathedral.

There is fine architecture to be seen all around the city, jealously guarded by the Limerick Civic Trust. The best old street is The Crescent, while modern architecture is superbly demonstrated in the Civic Centre and City Hall on Merchant's Quay.

✚ 48C2

Hunt Museum

✉ Custom House, Rutland Street

☎ 061-312833; www.huntmuseum.com

🕐 Mon–Sat 10–5, Sun 2–5

🍴 Restaurant (€€)

🚌 All city centre buses

♿ Very good

💷 Expensive

King John's Castle

✚ Nicholas Street, King's Island

☎ 061-360788

🕐 Apr–Oct daily 10–5:30; Nov–Mar 10:30–4:30

♿ Very good

💷 Expensive

Did you know ?

The first Waterford Glass factory was opened by George and William Penrose in 1783 and some of their work can be seen in Waterford City Hall, but the factory soon closed down, only to reopen in 1947. There is a gallery, and tours of the factory include the furnaces, glass blowing, annealing and cutting.

WATERFORD ⭐⭐

Waterford grew from an ancient Viking settlement into the foremost port in Ireland, and its quays are still busy with international trade; the famous **Waterford Crystal Visitor Centre** reflects this. The city preserves an atmosphere of the past, and the mixture of Celt, Viking, Norman, English, Flemish and Huguenot gives a European flavour which is reflected on the sea front and in its narrow lanes. One of the oldest buildings is Reginald's Tower, built by the Vikings in 1003, which now houses the city museum. The Church of Ireland cathedral is regarded as the finest 18th-century ecclesiastical building in Ireland, and the Catholic cathedral has a wonderful interior, with superb carving and stained glass.

✚ 49D2

Waterford Crystal Visitor Centre

✉ Kilbarry

☎ 051-332500

🕐 Visitor centre and shop: Mar–Oct daily 9–6; Nov–Feb daily 9–5. Tours: Mar–Oct daily 9–4:15, Nov–Feb Mon–Fri 9–3:15

🍴 Restaurant (€–€€)

🚌 Waterford–Ballybeg

♿ Good 💷 Expensive

Spectacular Scenery in Kerry & Cork

This drive includes the wonderful wooded mountains of the Killarney National Park, the spectacular Healy Pass and two of Ireland's finest historic houses.

From Killarney take the N71, signposted to Muckross, and soon reach the Killarney National Park and Muckross House (➤ 23).

Muckross' situation amid the mountains and lakes of the national park is unsurpassed.

Continue on the N71, passing Torc Waterfall, to reach Ladies View, then after 6km, at Molls Gap, bear left, signposted to Kenmare, Glengarriff. At Kenmare drive up the main street and turn right, then leave the town following signs for Glengarriff and Bantry. Cross a river bridge and turn right, signposted Castletown Bearhaven R571. Continue for about 14km then follow signs for Healy Pass.

This pass across the Caha Mountains has stunning views and a breathtaking summit.

Over the top of the pass, descend a series of hairpin bends and continue to reach a T-junction. Turn left for Glengarriff or right to lunch in Castletownbere.

Garinish Island, with its beautiful sub-tropical gardens, can be reached by ferry from Glengarriff.

Continue for 5.6km to Bantry.

By the harbour on the Cork road is Bantry House (➤ 52) and the Armada Exhibition.

Retrace the route to Glengarriff, then take the N71 to Kenmare and Killarney.

Distance
140km

Time
6–7 hours depending on attractions visited

Start/end point
Killarney
➕ 48B2

Lunch
The Copper Kettle (€)
✉ The Square, Castletownbere
☎ 027-71792
🕐 Mon–Sat

Ladies View is a spectacular viewpoint high above the Killarney National Park

59

The West

The wild beauty of the west is underlaid with the hostility of a landscape that does its best to defy cultivation. There are fields, but they are the size of pocket handkerchiefs, and the drystone walls that enclose them have by no means used up all of the land's loose rocks. Vast empty areas of blanket bog have pockets of wetness that expand into a network of lakes and rivers beneath the mountains of Connemara and Joyce's Country. The great Loughs – Conn, Mask and Corrib – lie between Sligo and Galway bays. Farther east the River Shannon forms the backbone of a watery highway. In Clare, The Burren is a moonscape of bare limestone, where plants cling on to the sparse soil, and the western boundary of all this is a jagged and spectacular coastline.

'I hear lake water lapping
with low sounds by
the shore…
I hear it in the deep
heart's core. '

W B YEATS
The Lake Isle of Innisfree (1893)

———————●———————

Looking towards Tully Mountain from Connemara National Park

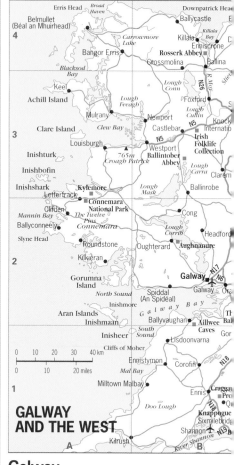

Erris Head *Broad Haven*
Downpatrick Hea
Belmullet
(Béal an Mhuirhead) Ballycastle E
Killala
Killala *Bay* D
Carrowmore *Lake*
Enniscrone
Bangor Erris Rosserk Abbey
Crossmolina Ballina
Blacksod Bay
Lough Conn
N26
Keel
Lough Feeagh
Foxford
Achill Island
Lough Cullin
Mulrany Newport
Knock
Clare Island *Clew Bay* Castlebar Internatio
Louisburgh N5
Irish Folklife
Inishturk Westport Collection
765m
Croagh Patrick Ballintober
Abbey
Lough Carra
Inishbofin Clarem
Lough Mask
Inishshark Kylemore Ballinrobe
Letterfrack
Clifden Connemara National Park
Cong
Mannín Bay The Twelve Pins
Ballyconneely Connemara *Lough Corrib*
Slyne Head Headford
Roundstone Oughterard Aughnanure
Kilkièran
K17
N6
Gorumna Island Galway
North Sound Spiddal Galway Or
Inishmore (An Spidéal) *G a l w a y B a y*
Aran Islands Galway
Inishmaan Ballyvaughan Th
South Sound Aillwee Ba
Inisheer Caves Gor
Lisdoonvarna
0 10 20 30 40 km *Cliffs of Moher*
Ennistymon Corofin
0   10   20 miles N18
Mal Bay
Milltown Malbay Ennis Cragga
Pro
GALWAY *Doo Lough*
Knappogue
AND THE WEST Sixmilebrid
Shannon N19 B
River Shannon
A Kilrush B

Galway

Galway, the historic capital of Connaught, is Ireland's fourth largest city, with a delightful blend of ancient and modern. Though it is surrounded by the urban sprawl of industry and superstores, it has at its heart a maze of narrow streets, lined with a mixture of modern shop fronts, traditional-style painted façades, old pubs and restaurants. A relaxed west coast atmosphere prevails, tempered by a lively student population.

Situated in the northeast corner of Galway Bay, where the River Corrib pours into the sea, Galway was built on international trade and sea fishing, and its oldest parts cluster

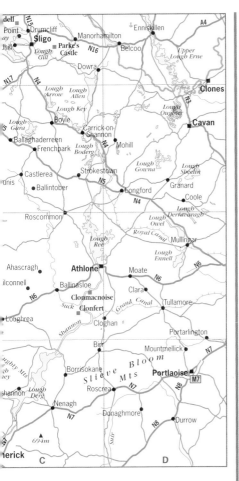

The harbour at Kilkieran is typical of Ireland's little fishing communities

around the harbour and riverside quays. On the east bank is the Spanish Arch, the city's most famous landmark, built to protect cargoes of wine and brandy from Iberia.

Behind the quay is a network of narrow streets, leading off from an equally narrow main thoroughfare. A modern shopping mall, incorporating part of the medieval city wall, is hidden away behind old façades.

On the far side of the river is The Claddagh, once a close-knit Gaelic-speaking fishing community and now remembered in the continuing tradition of the Claddagh ring, with two hands holding a crowned heart.

Salthill is Galway's seaside resort suburb, to the west, offering a good range of amusements and a popular long sandy beach.

What to See in Galway

CATHEDRAL OF OUR LADY ASSUMED INTO HEAVEN AND ST NICHOLAS ⭐

Overlooking the River Corrib near the Salmon Weir Bridge, this splendid modern Roman Catholic **cathedral** opened in 1965 and looked so grand that the locals dubbed it the 'Taj Michael', after the then Bishop of Galway, Michael (pronounced Mee-hawl) Brown.

Built on the site of the former county gaol, it's topped by a great copper dome, and the interior is plain but impressive, with floors of Connemara marble, rough-hewn limestone walls and superb stained glass. It was designed by John J Robinson and replaced the old cathedral on Abbeygate Street, which has been converted into shops.

NORA BARNACLE HOUSE MUSEUM ⭐

Built around the end of the 19th century, this tiny cottage, in a quiet street close to the city centre, now houses one of the smallest museums in Ireland. It was formerly the home of the eponymous Nora Barnacle, companion, wife and lifelong inspiration of the writer James Joyce. Even without the collections of memorabilia, it is impossible to ignore the romantic associations. Here, in 1909, Joyce first met Nora's mother, and the house now contains many letters, photographs and exhibits devoted to the couple.

ST NICHOLAS'S CHURCH ⭐

St Nicholas's Church is the largest medieval parish church in Ireland still in constant use. It was built around 1320 by the Lynch family and consecrated to the patron saint of sailors. Christopher Columbus worshipped here in 1477, and was no doubt inspired by tales of St Brendan the Navigator, an Irish monk who sailed to America in the 6th century. Outside the church, on the site of the former college, there is a colourful weekly Saturday market where crafts, organic vegetables and food are sold. In addition to its regular services, St Nicholas's hosts concerts throughout the year.

Christopher Columbus is said to have prayed in Galway's church of St Nicholas

A Walk Around Galway

From Eyre Square, the heart of the city, walk along William Street, Shop Street and High Street. Reach a cobbled crossroads and keep forward along Quay Street.

On the corner is Thomas Dillon's Claddagh Gold, a little jeweller's shop with a Claddagh Ring Museum in the back room. At the end is the famous Spanish Arch, where Iberian traders would land their cargoes, behind which is the new Galway City Museum.

Take the riverside path that leads off between the bridge and Jury's Hotel. Cross the next road and continue alongside the river on your left, and a canal on your right. At the end of the path, cross a footbridge over the canal, then turn left and walk to the Salmon Weir Bridge. Cross the bridge and the Cathedral of Our Lady Assumed into Heaven and St Nicholas is immediately ahead.

The Cathedral, completed in 1965, is topped by a great copper dome. The interior is light, spacious and, though plain, is still very impressive.

Recross the bridge and turn right down Newtown Smith, passing the footbridge crossed earlier. Keep forward, turn right at the crossroads, then at the end bear left. About halfway along on the right is the Nora Barnacle House Museum.

This tiny cottage is where the writer James Joyce courted his future wife. Mementoes of the couple are on display.

At the end, opposite St Nicholas Church, turn left into Market Street, then right into Upper Abbeygate Street.

The building at the end, on the right, is Lynch's Castle, now occupied by the Allied Irish Bank.

Turn left into William Street and return to Eyre Square.

Distance
About 2km

Time
2–3 hours

Start/end point
Eyre Square
🚌 All city centre buses

Lunch
McDonagh's Seafood House
(€–€€€)
✉ 22 Quay Street
☎ 091-565001
🕐 Seafood Bar: Mon–Sat
   12–9:45, Sun from 5PM
   (2PM in summer).
   Fish and chips: daily
   12–midnight (Sun 11–5)

What to See in The West

ARAN ISLANDS (► 16, TOP TEN)

BUNRATTY CASTLE AND FOLK PARK ✪✪✪

Bunratty, 14.5km northeast of Limerick, is Ireland's most complete medieval castle, thanks to the superb restoration work done in 1960 when the former ruin was purchased by Bord Failte and Lord Gort. Following the restoration, Lord Gort installed his collections of furniture, *objets d'art*, paintings and tapestries, all of which predate 1650. The castle has become famous for its medieval banquets, with historic costume and traditional food and entertainment.

In the castle grounds, Irish village life at the turn of the century has been re-created, with reconstructed urban and rural dwellings, farmhouses, a watermill, forge and village street, complete with shops and a pub – all brought to life by knowledgeable costumed guides. The restored Regency walled garden opened in June 2000.

THE BURREN AND AILLWEE CAVE ✪✪✪

The Burren National Park preserves a remarkable landscape that continues to excite geologists and botanists from far and wide. It is a vast plateau of limestone hills which were scraped free of their soil by retreating glaciers 15,000 years ago, then eroded by rain and Atlantic mists. The tiny amounts of soil that gather in the rock fissures

Sidebar:

➕ 62B1
✉ N18 Bunratty
☎ 061-360788
🕐 Daily 9–5:30 (until 6 Jun–Aug). Last admission 45 minutes before closing
🍴 Tea room (€); lunches in barn May–Oct (€); Mac's Pub (€€)
🚌 From Limerick, Ennis and Galway
🚆 Limerick and Ennis
♿ Park good; castle poor
💶 Expensive

➕ 62B2

Burren Exposure
✉ Ballyvaughan
☎ 065-7077277
🕐 Mar–Nov daily 9–6

support both Alpine and Mediterranean plant life, and early summer is the main flowering season. **The Burren Exposure** visitors' centre provides an overview of the area and its unique landscape, its human history and its famous flora. **Aillwee Cave**, south of Ballyvaughan, has fossil formations and water figures. The Burren is best appreciated on foot, and the waymarked 42km Burren Way, running from Ballyvaughan and Liscannor, can be undertaken in short sections.

CASTLEBAR ⊗

Castlebar is the county town of County Mayo. Its most notable attraction is the new Irish folklife collection. Housed in a carefully renovated 18th-century building, along with purpose-built extensions and grounds, this is the first branch of the National Museum to be located outside Dublin. Innovative displays, utilising 50,000 items – crafts, household utensils, tools and clothing – reflect the lives of Ireland's people and their trades, illustrating the social history of Ireland over the past 200 years.

CLIFFS OF MOHER ⊗⊗⊗

These towering cliffs rise sheer out of the turbulent Atlantic to a height of nearly 213m and stretch for 8km along the Clare coast north of Hag's Head. Majestic in calm weather, the cliffs are most dramatic (and dangerous) when stormy seas crash into their base, hurling pebbles high up into the air. Horizontal layers of flagstones have been exposed by coastal erosion, making convenient perches for the sea birds, including puffins, which abound here. At the highest point of the cliffs, **O'Brien's Tower** (closed until 2007) was built in the early 19th century as a lookout point for tourists, and gives views of the Clare Coastline, the Aran Islands and mountains as far apart as Kerry and Connemara. It now includes a visitor centre.

CLONMACNOISE (▶ 18, TOP TEN)

Aillwee Cave
- ✉ Ballyvaughan
- ☎ 065-7077036
- ⏰ Tours only, daily from 10, last tour 5:30 (Jul–Aug until 6), Dec by appointment only

➕ 62B3

Museum of Country Life
- ✉ Turlough Park House
- ☎ 094-9031755; www.museum.ie
- ⏰ Tue–Sat 10–5, Sun 2–5
- 🍴 Restaurant
- 🎫 Free

➕ 62B1

O'Brien's Tower and Visitor Centre
- ✉ Near Liscannor
- ☎ 065-7081565
- ⏰ Closed for restoration until 2007
- 🚌 From Lahinch and other nearby towns
- ♿ First viewing platform accessible to wheelchairs
- 🎫 Cheap; nearby car parking €4 per car

Two geological marvels of County Clare: the Burren, opposite, and (above) the towering Cliffs of Moher

✚ 62A2

National Park Visitor Centre
✉ Letterfrack
☎ 095-41054
🕐 Jul–Aug daily 9:30–6; Jun 10–6; Sep to mid-Oct, Apr–May 10–5:30
🍴 Tea rooms (€)
♿ Good 💷 Cheap
❓ Guided walks Jun–Aug; programme of talks and special events for children

CONNEMARA ❃❃❃

To the northwest of Galway City is Connemara, with some of the most dramatic scenery in Ireland. Much of its convoluted coastline, with masses of tiny islands and some excellent beaches, can be followed by road – narrow and bumpy for the most part, so do not expect to get anywhere fast – and the views are spectacular. Inland, in southern Connemara, are thousands of lakes amid the bogland. Further north, and hardly ever out of sight, are the brooding ranges of the Twelve Pins and the Maumturk Mountains. Connemara Marble is quarried at Recess, and there is a factory shop and showroom at Connemara Marble Industries in Moycullen.

A landscape laced with glittering lakes near Screeb, Connemara

The Connemara National Park protects about 2,000 hectares of the mountains, bogs, heaths and grasslands, and there is a good visitor centre in Letterfrack, with exhibitions, audio-visuals, nature trails, information – and a herd of Connemara ponies.

✚ 62B1
✉ Kilmurry, near Quin
☎ 061-360788
🕐 Apr–Oct daily 9:30–5 (last admission 1 hour before closing)
♿ Few
💷 Moderate
❓ Medieval banquets on demand

KNAPPOGUE CASTLE ❃❃

Built in the mid-15th century for the MacNamaras, Knappogue underwent many changes over the course of the next five centuries. It was extended and adapted and used as government offices for a while, before falling into a ruinous state. In the 1960s it was acquired by Mark Edwin Andrews, then Assistant Secretary to the US Navy. He and his wife set about the task of restructuring the castle into an authentic setting for the medieval banquets which continue to be popular. They include dinner and a pageant, with stories of the history of the women of Ireland – real and legendary. The castle was acquired by the Shannon Development Company in 1996.

KYLEMORE ABBEY ✪✪

Kylemore Abbey's greatest attraction is its location. Nestled at the base of Duchruach Mountain, and on the north shores of Lough Pollacapul in the heart of the Connemara Mountains, it is regarded as one of Ireland's most romantic buildings. Lying in a rhododendron filled hollow, this neo-Gothic estate castle was constructed for British shipping magnate and Irish politican Mitchell Henry. Since 1920 it has been a convent of the Irish Benedictine nuns, and a girls' boarding school now occupies the building. It offers the warmth and hospitality of its peaceful setting to visitors from all over the world. The restaurant has the best of home cooking and a range of the abbey's distinctive pottery can be seen in the studio. Within the grounds there is a gothic chapel, which has a Connemara marble interior. Nearby is a *Taghallai*, a pre-Christian tomb. The 2.5ha restored Victorian walled garden is well worth a visit, as is the visitor centre.

THE SHANNON ✪✪

Ireland's longest river, the Shannon rises in a humble pool (called the Shannon Pot) in County Cavan, then gathers strength as it flows through a series of lakes before it meets the Atlantic beyond Limerick. Historically, river crossings were always points where towns grew and prospered – places such as Carrick-on-Shannon and Athlone, which are bases for the leisure cruiser holidays for which this mighty river is so popular. Anglers, too, find this river rewarding for its variety of fish.

🞢 62A3
✉ Connemara
☎ 095-41146
ℹ Visitor Centre: Mar–Nov daily 9:30–5:30; Nov–Mar daily 10:30–4; gardens mid-Mar to Oct 9:30–5:30. Closed Christmas week and Good Friday
🍴 Tearoom (€–€€)
🚌 No bus
♿ Good
💰 Expensive

Athlone Castle, on the River Shannon

🞢 62B1
ℹ Shannon Development (☎ 061-361555)

Westport House is one of the greatest attractions in northwest Ireland

+ 63C4
i Temple Street (☎ 071-
9161201); www.
irelandnorthwest.ie

SLIGO ⭕⭕

Sligo is a lively and attractive town with splendid old shop-fronts and traditional music pubs. It is also a significant cultural centre and has a fine range of art galleries and museums, as well as the various festivals which take place throughout the year.

Over 1,000 years of history have shaped the town, but it is literature that attracts many of its visitors. This is Yeats country, and the subject of one of his best-known poems is just outside the town – the Isle of Inisfree in Lough Gill (riverboat trips to the lough depart from Sligo's Doorly Park). Sligo has many other attractions including two fine cathedrals and Sligo Abbey, a Dominican friary founded in 1252.

+ 62B3
Westport House
✉ The Quay, Westport
☎ 098-25430/27766;
www.westporthouse.ie
🕐 Jul–Oct daily 11:30–5;
Apr–Jun, Sat–Mon
11:30–5; Nov Sat–Sun
11:30–5
🍴 Café Jun, Aug only (€)
♿ Few
💷 Expensive

WESTPORT ⭕⭕

Set on Clew Bay, Westport is one of the liveliest and most charming towns in the west of Ireland, with broad Georgian streets and a leafy riverside avenue at its heart. Nearby **Westport House** dates from the 1730s and has wholeheartedly embraced its role as the only stately home open to the public in Sligo. It is beautifully furnished and has some superb Waterford crystal, silver and paintings. The dungeons are from an earlier building, reputedly a castle of Grace O'Malley, the 16th-century pirate queen.

The grounds contain many rides and amusements for children, including an thrilling log flume.

+ 62B2
✉ Gort
☎ 091-631436, off season
091-537700
🕐 May–Sep daily 10–6
♿ Few
💷 Moderate
❓ Audio-visual presentation
and displays of first
editions. Bookshop, craft
centre, picnic area

YEATS TOWER, THOOR BALLYLEE ⭕⭕

In 1917 the poet William Butler Yeats bought this derelict 16th-century tower house and renovated it. For the next 12 years he and his family spent their summers here and it was in these peaceful surroundings that he wrote most of his works. His friend and patron, Lady Gregory, lived near by, and together they were the inspiration behind the Irish Literary Revival and the founding of the Abbey Theatre in Dublin. In the 1960s Thoor Ballylee was again restored, to show how it looked when Yeats was here, and, when completed, was opened to the public.

The Coast, Lakes & Mountains of Connemara

This drive follows the coastline for much of the way, with views of the Aran Islands in the early stages. It then passes through isolated settlements amid a rocky landscape, with mountain views, to end at the lovely little town of Clifden.

From Galway follow signs for Salthill until a roundabout on the seafront, then take the Spiddal road west along Galway Bay. At the T-junction turn left, signposted Carraroe and Barna, then after about 13km pass through Spiddal.

Distance
112km

Time
About 5 hours, including stop for lunch and visits to craft workshops

Start point
Galway
✚ 62B2

End point
Clifden
✚ 62A2

Lunch
O'Dowds Seafood Restaurant
(€€–€€€)
✉ Roundstone
☎ 095-35809

There are breathtaking views along the coast and across Galway Bay before the road swings right to open up an inland vista of distant mountains.

Turn right on to the R336, signed 'Cill Ciarain, Scriob, Carna and Ros Muc', then after 11.2km at a T-junction, make a left turn signed 'Connemara Scenic Route'. Continue through Cill Ciarain (Kilkieran), then after 8.4km bear right, signed 'Clifden', with views of the Twelve Pins ahead. Turn left on to the R342 and follow signs for Roundstone.

This charming village is the home of Malachy Kearns' *bodhrán* workshop, where the craftsman can often be seen making his famous traditional Irish drums. There is also a pottery close by.

After 13.2km reach Ballyconneely and continue around the rocky bay, then turn left into Clifden after a further 9.2km.

A romantic neo-Gothic mansion in a wonderful setting, Kylemore Abbey is now a girls' convent school

If you want to complete the circle, the road back to Galway (about 48km) is straightforward and well signposted, passing through magnificent scenery.

The North

When Brendan Behan said 'there is no such thing as bad publicity' he could not have contemplated the task of promoting the six counties of Northern Ireland (sometimes referred to as Ulster) as a tourist destination. The Province's unfortunate reputation deters many, and this is a great shame because they are missing some of the most beautiful scenery in Europe. The coast of Antrim offers a spectacular drive past the lovely Glens before swinging to the west to the Giant's Causeway. Further south the Mountains of Mourne sweep down to the sea. Inland are forest parks, lakes and mountains, historic towns, ancient sites and, of course, Belfast, a busy city with an industrial heritage and a lively arts scene. This section also includes the far north-western part of the Republic, Co Donegal, famous for its beaches and tweed.

> *'England and Ireland may flourish together. The world is large enough for us both. Let it be our care not to make ourselves too little for it.'*

EDMUND BURKE
Letter to Samuel Span, Esq (1778)

———————●———————

The harbour at Annalong with the Mourne Mountains in the distance

Belfast

The capital of Northern Ireland is a relatively young city that grew rapidly in Victorian times, when its linen and shipbuilding industries flourished and the city doubled in size every 10 years. Today it has a unique character, brought about by the culmination of hard work, hard times and a particular brand of Irish humour. The redevelopment of its dockyard areas continues to breathe new life and prosperity into the eastern flank of the city centre.

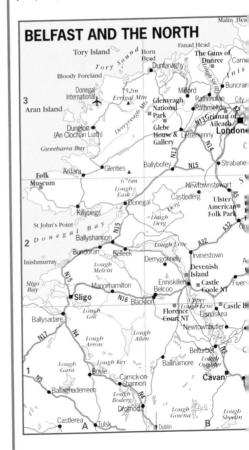

BELFAST AND THE NORTH

Belfast's industrial past, together with the disturbing images of the recent troubles, can conjure up a somewhat misleading picture for those who have never visited the city. Its Victorian prosperity has left a legacy of magnificent public buildings and monuments, finance houses and warehouses.

At the heart of the city is the spacious and leafy Donegall Square, dominated by the magnificent City Hall, and surrounded by the main shopping streets – the whole area is being rejunvenated. Belfast has superb museums, libraries and art galleries, excellent shopping and a lively and varied cultural life, from grand opera to informal traditional music sessions. Beautiful parks and gardens include the famous Botanic Gardens and the canalside Lagan Valley Regional Park, but the most spectacular is on the slopes of Cave Hill to the north, which incorporates the zoo, Belfast Castle and a heritage centre.

A detail of the ornate
exterior of Belfast's
Grand Opera House

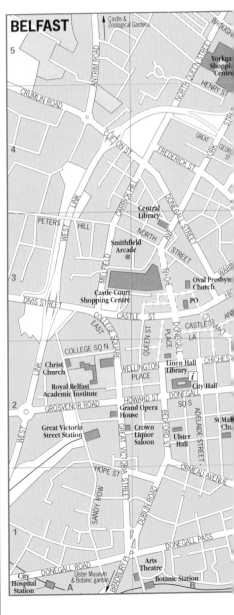

BELFAST

↑ Castle &
Zoological Gardens

Yorkgate
Shopping
Centre

HENRY ST

ANTRIM ROAD

CRUMLIN ROAD

NORTH QUEEN STREET

BROUGH

CLIFTON ST

FREDERICK ST

GREAT

GEORGE ST

CORK ST

LINK

CARRICK HILL

DONEGALL STREET

Central
Library

PETERS

WEST

HILL

NORTH

ROYAL

STREET

AVE

Smithfield
Arcade

MILLFIELD

Oval Presbyterian
Church

WARD

DIVIS STREET

Castle Court
Shopping Centre

CASTLE ST

PO

HI

COLLEGE

CORNMKT

CASTLE

LA

DONEGALL PLACE

AND

EAST

SQUARE

QUEEN ST

COLLEGE SQ N

WELLINGTON
PLACE

Linen Hall
Library

CHICHES

LINK

Christ
Church

i

City Hall

Royal Belfast
Academic Institute

HOWARD ST

DONEGALL
SQ S

GROSVENOR ROAD

Grand Opera
House

BEDFORD ST

ADELAIDE STREET

St Malachy's
Church

WEST

Great Victoria
Street Station

GREAT VICTORIA STREET

Crown
Liquor
Saloon

Ulster
Hall

ORMEAU AVENUE

HOPE ST

SANDY ROW

DUBLIN ROAD

DONEGALL PASS

City
Hospital
Station

DONEGALL ROAD

Ulster Museum
& Botanic garden

Arts
Theatre

BRADBURY PL

A

Botanic Station

B

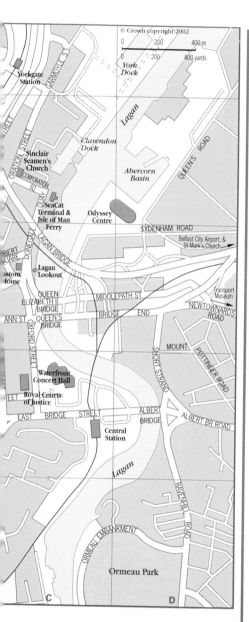

© Crown copyright 2002

York Dock

Yorkgate Station

Lagan

Clarendon Dock

Sinclair Seamen's Church

Abercorn Basin

QUEEN'S ROAD

SeaCat Terminal & Isle of Man Ferry

Odyssey Centre

SYDENHAM ROAD

Belfast City Airport, & St Mark's Church

Custom House

Lagan Lookout

QUEEN ELIZABETH II BRIDGE

MIDDLEPATH ST

Transport Museum

ANN ST

QUEEN'S BRIDGE

BRIDGE END

NEWTOWNARDS ROAD

OXFORD STREET

MOUNT

POTTINGER ROAD

Waterfront Concert Hall

Royal Courts of Justice

SHORT STRAND

EAST BRIDGE STREET

ALBERT BRIDGE

ALBERT BR ROAD

Central Station

Lagan

RAVENHILL ROAD

ORMEAU EMBANKMENT

Ormeau Park

C   D

The splendid Victorian palm house at Belfast Botanic Garden

Sidebar information

✚ 76A1
✉ Stranmillis Road
☎ 028 9032 4902
🕐 Daily. Palm House:
Apr–Sep Mon–Fri 10–5,
Sat–Sun 2–5; Oct–Mar
Mon–Fri 10–4, Sat–Sun
2–4. Closes for lunch
🚌 84, 85
🚆 Botanic Station
♿ Good 🎟 Free

Ulster Museum
☎ 028 9038 3000
🕐 Mon–Fri 10–5, Sat 1–5,
Sun 2–5 🎟 Free

✚ 76B2
✉ Donegall Square
☎ 028 9027 0456
🕐 Tours: Jun–Sep Mon–Fri
11, 2, 3, Sat 2:30;
Oct–May Mon–Fri 11,
2:30, Sat 2:30
♿ Good 🎟 Free

✚ 76A2
✉ Great Victoria Street
☎ 028 9027 9901
🕐 Licensing hours
♿ Few
🎟 Free

✚ 77C3
✉ Donegall Quay
☎ 028 9031 5444
🕐 Apr–Sep Mon–Fri 11–5,
Sat noon–5, Sun 2–5;
Oct–Mar Tue–Fri
11–3:30, Sat 1–4:30,
Sun 2–4:30
♿ Good 🎟 Cheap

✚ 77D4
✉ 2 Queen's Quay
☎ 028 9045 1055
♿ Good
🎟 Varies by attraction

What to See in Belfast

BOTANIC GARDEN ✪✪✪
The Botanic Garden is a wonderful place to wander away from the bustle of the city. It includes a fragrant rose garden, formal beds and herbaceous borders, and among the outstanding greenhouses is the Palm House. Begun in 1839, it is a remarkable cast-iron curvilinear structure in which tropical flowering plants thrive. Also in these lovely surroundings, the **Ulster Museum** gives a fascinating insight into the life and history of the Province. 'Made in Belfast' underlines the industry and inventiveness of Ulster (Northern Ireland) people, and there are displays on dinosaurs, armada treasures, the flora and fauna of Ireland and 'Early Ireland' (10000 BC–1500 BC)

CITY HALL ✪✪
In 1906 Belfast's City Hall was completed to mark the granting of city status by Queen Victoria. Set around a central courtyard, the building, of Portland stone, is topped by a tall copper dome which rises above the central staircase at the heart of an exuberant interior of rich mosaic, stained glass, marble and wood panelling.

CROWN LIQUOR SALOON ✪✪
High Victorian décor is preserved in this restored pub, in the care of the National Trust. It's a working pub managed by a brewery. The tiled exterior, with Corinthian pillars flanking the doorway, gives way to marble counters, stained glass, gleaming brass and ornately carved 'snugs'.

LAGAN LOOKOUT ✪✪
Urban regeneration continues to progress in the 3-mile stretch of riverside known as Laganside. The £14 million Lagan Weir enabled a big clean-up of the river and Lagan Lookout tells the story of the project, including the history of the area and future plans. Visitors can see the weir, view the *Titanic* display, use interactive terminals and take a close-up look at one of the city's newest icons – the 10m ceramic salmon, *The Big Fish*, by local sculptor, John Kindness.

ODYSSEY ✪
Belfast's big millennium project was the building of this complex covering 23 acres of the riverfront. It includes an interactive science centre with a special area for the under eights, an IMAX theatre, a 12-screen multiplex cinema and a huge arena, and the Pavilion has restaurants, bars and shops.

A Walk Around Belfast

This walk starts in the heart of the city, then heads south along 'The Golden Mile' to visit the lovely Botanic Garden and the splendid Ulster Museum.

Donegall Square is surrounded by splendid architecture. Take a look at some of the statues and monuments in the grounds of City Hall before going inside (guided tours can be arranged in advance).

Leave by the exit on the opposite side. Outside the gates of City Hall turn left along Donegall Square South. At the corner cross into May Street, then turn right into Alfred Street. Continue to reach St Malachy's on the left.

St Malachy's was built in 1844 in castellated Gothic style with dark red brick and slender octagonal turrets. Inside there is fine fan-vaulting and an organ by Telford.

From St Malachy's go forward into Clarence Street, turn left into Bedford Street, then bear right into Dublin Street and continue to Shaftesbury Square. Continue along Bradbury Place and fork left into University Road. Beyond the university, turn left to enter the Botanic Garden, where the Ulster Museum can be found.

The beautiful Botanic Garden features a great Palm House and Tropical Ravine. Near by is the excellent Ulster Museum.

Retrace your steps to Shaftesbury Square, then fork left to go along Great Victoria Street, passing the Crown Liquor Saloon on the right.

Try to time the walk so that this famous National Trust pub, with its sumptuous and ornate Victorian interior, will be open.

Continue past the Europa Hotel and the splendid Opera House, then turn right into Howard Street and return to Donegall Square.

Distance
About 4km

Time
3–4 hours, including cathedral, garden and museum visits

Start/end point
Donegall Square
🚌 76B2
🚍 All city centre buses

Lunch
Crown Liquor Saloon (££)
✉ Great Victoria Street
☎ 028 9027 9901

The Crown Liquor Saloon is a wonderful piece of living history

Splendidly imposing St Patrick's RC Cathedral contains the red hats of the cardinal archbishops of Armagh

What to See in The North

ARMAGH ✪✪✪

Armagh is a distinguished city with a heritage of national importance. Nearby Navan Fort was the ancient capital of the kings of Ulster, and in AD 445 St Patrick built his first church on the site now occupied by St Patrick's Cathedral. From here the Irish were converted to Christianity and Armagh remains the ecclesiastical capital of Ireland. There has been much rebuilding of this Church of Ireland cathedral, but its core is medieval. There is also a Roman Catholic cathedral of St Patrick, finished in 1904, with a lavish interior of murals depicting Irish saints. **St Patrick's Trian**, in English Street, has an exhibition on the saint,

> ### *Did you know ?*
>
> *St Patrick was born about AD 390 in Britain, the son of a Romano–British official. At 16 he was kidnapped by pirates and sold into slavery in Ireland, but later escaped with, he claimed, divine intervention. This prompted his training for the ministry in Britain, before returning to Ireland and establishing the Christian faith there.*

along with the Land of Lilliput featuring Gulliver's travels.

The city has many other beautiful buildings in the old streets, and the stables of the former Archbishop's Palace have been converted into the excellent **Palace Stables Heritage Centre**.

BALLYCASTLE ✪✪✪

Ballycastle, Co Antrim's largest town, is a popular seaside resort surrounded by some of Ireland's loveliest scenery. Near by is the Carrick-a-Rede Rope Bridge, suspended

 75C2
🚌 From Portadown Station
🚏 Portadown

St Patrick's Trian
✉ 40 English Street
☎ 028 3752 1801; www.saintpatrickstrian.com
🕐 Mon–Sat 10–5, Sun 2–5
🍴 Restaurant (£)
♿ Good
💷 Moderate

Palace Stables Heritage Centre
✉ Friary Road
☎ 028 3752 9629
🕐 Apr–Sep Sat–Sun 10–5
🍴 Coffee shop (£), restaurant (£)
♿ Good
💷 Moderate

🗺 75D3
🚌 From Ballymoney Station
🚏 Ballymoney

24.5m above the sea, linking the clifftop to a rocky island, and from the harbour there are trips to Rathlin Island, one of the best places for birdwatching in Ireland. On the edge of the town are the ruins of **Bonamargy Friary**, founded around 1500 and the burial place of the MacDonnell chiefs. At the end of August each year, the Diamond at the centre of the town is crammed with the stalls, entertainments and horse-dealing of the famous Oul' Lammas Fair. **The Ballycastle Museum** is housed in the 18th-century courthouse, and there is a Seafront Exhibition Centre with crafts and information.

CARRICKFERGUS ⚫⚫
Carrickfergus has the country's finest Norman **castle**, constructed on the edge of the sea in the late 12th century and still in use (as a magazine and armoury) as recently as 1928. Its impressive walls now house three floors of exhibitions and a medieval fair is held here each July.

There are remains of the 17th-century town walls, the earliest and largest urban defence in Ulster, including the North Gate which has been rebuilt and restored.

Carrickfergus was the first footfall in Ireland of William of Orange, who landed at the harbour in 1690 for his victorious campaign against James II. Billy's Rock reputedly marks the exact spot.

Visit the unusual **Flame! The Gasworks Museum of Ireland**, Ireland's sole surviving coal gasworks that supplied the town with gas for over 100 years until 1967.

DONEGAL ⚫⚫
Donegal Tweed has made the name of this northwest corner of Ireland familiar all around the world. It is a modest little town, but it has the remains of two castles and two abbeys, and is attractively set at the head of Donegal Bay. **Donegal Castle**, on the banks of the River Eske in the town centre, was built in 1505 for Red Hugh O'Donnell and was considerably enlarged in the 17th century for Sir Basil Brooke. The Brooke family also owned Lough Eske Castle, a Jacobean-style house which was damaged by fire in 1939.

South of the town is **Donegal Abbey**. *The Annals of the Four Masters* was written here in the 17th century; charting the history of Ireland up until 1616. This important chronicle is now in the National Library in Dublin.

Bonamargy Friary
- ✉ Ballycastle
- 🕐 All year
- ♿ Few
- 🎟 Free

Ballycastle Museum
- ✉ 59 Castle Street
- ☎ 028 2076 2942
- 🕐 Jul–Aug (or by arrangement) Mon–Sat 12–6
- ♿ Good
- 🎟 Free

Intrepid visitors cross the Carrick-a-Rede Rope Bridge

- ➕ 75D2
- 🚌 Carrickfergus

Carrickfergus Castle
- ✉ Marine Highway
- ☎ 028 9335 1273
- 🕐 Apr, May, Sep Mon–Sat 10–6, Sun 2–6; Jun–Aug Mon–Sat 10–6, Sun 12–6; Oct–Mar Mon–Sat 10–4, Sun 2–4
- ♿ Good 🎟 Moderate

Flame!
- ✉ 44 Irish Quarter West
- ☎ 028 9336 9575
- 🕐 Apr–Jun, Sep daily 2–6; Jul–Aug 10–6; Mar, Oct Sat–Sun 2–6 🎟 Cheap

---
- ➕ 74A2

Donegal Castle
- ✉ Tinchonaill Street
- ☎ 074-9722405
- 🕐 Mid-Mar to Nov, daily 10–6 (last admission 45mins before closing)
- 🎟 Moderate

Donegal Abbey
- ✉ Donegal
- ☎ Call Donegal tourist office: 074-9721148
- 🕐 Daily
- 🍴 Refreshments (€)

In the Know

If you only have a short time to visit Ireland, or would like to get a real flavour of the country, here are some ideas:

10 Ways To Be A Local

Relax – the local saying is that God created time, then he gave the Irish more of it.

Talk – strike up conversation wherever you go. No Irish person would walk into an occupied room without saying something to someone.

Do not take things too seriously – the Irish are renowned for their sense of humour and storytelling.

Develop a taste for Guinness – it somehow makes you feel you belong. And be patient – it takes a long time to pour a good pint.

Be subtle – the Irish tend not to be loud and brash, so make your enquiries soft and your conversation easy.

Be genuine – the Irish are usually really interested in what you have to say.

Know how to let your hair down – that laid-back attitude seems to evaporate when the time comes to have a 'hooley'.

Forget the old Hollywood myths and stereotypes – there may be a degree of unsophistication in the rural areas, but the Irish are generally outward-looking and forward-thinking.

Do not mind the weather – though Ireland has a mild climate, there is a strong possibility that you will be rained on at some point. Head for a cosy bar and wait for the sun to reappear.

Forget your diet – the Irish know how to fill a plate, particularly at breakfast time, and it all tastes too good to pass up.

10 Good Places To Have Lunch

Ahernes (€–€€) ✉ 163 North Main Street, Youghal, Co Cork ☎ 024-92424. Plenty of awards have been won by this charming restaurant.

Ballymaloe House (€€) ✉ Shanagarry Midleton, Co Cork ☎ 021-4652531. You could hardly fail to get a good lunch here, at the home of the Ballymaloe Cookery School. Local produce is used to produce excellent, good-value food.

Eccles Hotel (€–€€) ✉ Glengarriff, Co Cork ☎ 027-63003. Charming Victorian hotel, where good food can be enjoyed while overlooking Bantry Bay.

The Edge (££) ✉ Mays Meadow, Laganbank Road, Belfast ☎ 028 9032 2000. Delectable dishes prepared with local produce. Views over River Lagan.

Harvey's Point (€€) ✉ Lough Eske, Donegal ☎ 074-9722208. Great food in a wonderful location on the edge of Lough Eske.

Nick's Warehouse (££) ✉ 35–39 Hill Street, Belfast ☎ 028 9043 9690. Superb food in a popular, modern venue. The open kitchen lets you watch the chefs at work.

The Oliver St John Gogarty (€€) ✉ 58–59 Fleet Street, Temple Bar, Dublin ☎ 01-671 1822. Traditional Irish food and a lively atmosphere in a historic pub at the heart of Temple Bar.

Paddy Burke's (€–€€) ✉ Clarenbridge, Co Galway ☎ 091-796226. Paddy Burke's is famous as the focal point of the popular Clarenbridge Oyster Festival, so it is not surprising that its speciality dish is shellfish.

Patrick Guilbaud (€€€) ✉ 21 Upper Merrion Street, Dublin

01-676 4192. One of the finest restaurants in the city offering superb classic French cuisine in elegant surroundings. Popular with business clients.

Ramore Wine Bar (££)
✉ The Harbour, Portrush, Co Antrim ☎ 028 7082 4313. A popular restaurant right on the harbour, offering excellent food and a good wine list.

10

Top Activities

- Angling
- Birdwatching
- Cruising on the Shannon or Erne waterways
- Cycling
- Going to a pub music session
- Golf
- Horse-racing
- Horse-riding
- Sailing
- Walking

10

Boat Trips

Cork Harbour from Cobh (Booking office: Marine Transport Services, Atlantic Quay, Cobh)

Dingle Bay and Fungi the Dolphin (Booking office: Dingle Bay Ferries, Dunromen, Lispole, Co Kerry)

Killarney Lakes from Ross Castle (Booking office: Killarney Watercoach Cruises, 3 High Street, Killarney, Co Kerry)

Lough Corrib and Inchagoill Island (Booking office: Tourist office, Eyre Square, Galway)

Lough Derg–Killaloe (Booking office: Derg Maine, Kilaloe, Co Clare)

Lough Key Forest Park (Booking office: Lough Key Boat Tours, Rockingham Harbour, Lough Key Forest Park, Boyle, Co Roscommon)

Lough Ree–Athlone (Booking office:, Shannon Holidays, Jolly Mariner, Maine, Athlone, Co Westmeath)

River Erne from Belturbet (Booking office: Tarbot Tours, Deanery Park, Belturbet, Co Cavan)

Skelligs from Valencia (Booking office: The Skellig Experience, Valencia Island, Co Kerry)

Waterford–Carrick-on-Suir Castle (Booking office: Gallery Cruising Restaurant, Bridge Quay, New Ross, Co Wexford)

10

Souvenir Ideas

- Aran knitwear
- Belleek pottery
- Claddagh rings
- Connemara marble
- Donegal tweed
- Irish linen
- Irish whiskey
- Limerick lace
- Peat carvings
- Waterford crystal

Above: *Ballina, Co Mayo, is a popular angling centre*
Left: *using traditional farming methods*

10

Events

- St Patrick's Day, Dublin, March
- Historic Sham Fight, Scarva, Co Down, July
- Oul' Lammas Fair, Ballycastle, Co Antrim. August
- Ballyshannon International Folk Festival, Co Donegal. August
- Cahersiveen Celtic Festival of Music and the Arts, Co Kerry. August
- Galway International Oyster Festival, Co Galway. September
- Storytelling Festival, Cape Clear, Co Cork. September
- Kinsale Gourmet Festival, Co Cork. October
- Wexford Opera Festival, Wexford, October.
- Belfast Arts Festival, November

🔶 74B2

🚢 Ferry from Lower Lough Erne, 5km north of Enniskillen, to Devenish Island

Enniskillen Castle

✉ Castle Barracks, Wellington Road

☎ 028 6632 5000

🕐 Mon 2–5, Tue–Fri 10–5. Also May–Sep Sat 2–5; Jul–Aug Sun 2–5

🚌 Ulster Bus Station

♿ Few 💷 Cheap

Castle Coole

☎ 028 6632 2690

🕐 Grounds: May–Sep daily 10–8; Oct–Apr daily 10–4. House: Mar to mid-May, Sep Sat–Sun 12–6; Jun–Aug daily 12–6 (closed Tue in Jun). Last tour 5:15

🍴 Refreshments (£)

🚌 Ulsterbus 261 from Belfast to Enniskillen

♿ Few 💷 Moderate

Florence Court

✉ 12km southwest of Enniskillen

☎ 028 6634 8249/8497

🕐 Grounds: May–Sep daily 10–8; Oct–Apr daily 10–4. House: Jun–Aug daily 12–6; rest of year Sat–Sun and public hols 12–6. Last tour 5:15

🍴 Tea room (£)

🚌 Ulsterbus 192 Enniskillen–Swanlinbar

♿ Good 💷 Moderate

🔶 75C3

Dunluce Castle

✉ 87 Dunluce Road, Bushmills

☎ 028 2073 1938

ENNISKILLEN ✪✪

Enniskillen is attractively set on the River Erne between Upper and Lower Lough Erne. **Enniskillen Castle**, built in early 15th century, was the medieval stronghold of the Maguires and has a picturesque water gate. The keep now houses the Fermanagh Museum and a military museum. St Macartan's Cathedral is a small but interesting building, dating from the early 17th century, with some fine monuments and stained glass.

The Fermanagh Lakelands surrounding Enniskillen provide for all kinds of water-based leisure pursuits, and on Devenish Island is an important monastic site, founded in the 6th century by St Molaise.

A little further afield is **Castle Coole**, a fine neo-classical house designed by James Wyatt in 1795. The interiors are exquisite and the lovely parkland runs down to the shores of Lough Coole. **Florence Court** is to the southwest, an 18th-century mansion noted for its rococo plasterwork.

Florence Court is magnificently set in mature parkland, part of which is now a Forest Park

THE GIANT'S CAUSEWAY (▶ 20–21, TOP TEN)

THE GIANT'S CAUSEWAY COAST ✪✪

The Giant's Causeway coast encompasses dramatic cliffs, wide sandy beaches, pretty fishing villages and clifftop castles. Portrush, the nearest large town, is a traditional seaside resort with two splendid beaches, and near by is **Dunluce Castle**, a fairytale ruin which seems to grow out of the rock on which it is perched. Portballintrae is a pretty fishing village, made famous by the discovery in 1967 of the most valuable sunken treasure ever found on an armada wreck – the *Girona* – which foundered here in 1588, with only five survivors from its 1,300 crew. The rescued treasure is now on display and can be seen in Belfast's Ulster Museum (▶ 84).

Apr, May, Sep Mon–Sat 10–5, Sun 2–6; Jun–Aug Mon–Sat 10–6, Sun 2–6; Oct–Mar Mon–Sat 10–4, Sun 2–4

172 Portrush–Ballycastle

Few   Cheap

William Thackeray described beautiful Glenariff as 'Switzerland in miniature'

THE GLENS OF ANTRIM   ●●●
There are nine Glens of Antrim, lying roughly east of an imaginary line drawn between Ballycastle and Ballymena, and all of them are beautiful. There are wide valleys with a patchwork of green pastures, densely wooded mountain slopes and rocky gorges with tumbling streams dappled by the sunlight shining through the overhanging trees. Many of the glens are designated nature reserves and there are splendid walks, rich in wildlife and botanical interest and often with views to the coast. Millions of years of geological upheaval have formed these delightful valleys, which lie between the great plateau of the Antrim Mountains and a coastline that is justifiably described as the most scenic in the British Isles (▶ 90). Glenariff, the best known, has been dubbed the 'queen of the glens', and there is a wonderful view from the visitor centre.

75C3/75D3

Tourist Information Centre: Sheskburn House, 7 Mary Street, Ballycastle (☎ 028 2076 2024)

LETTERKENNY   ●
Letterkenny is on the River Swilly, with the lovely Fanad and Inishowen peninsulas to the north, and the Glenveagh National Park and Derryveagh Mountains to the west.

Letterkenny's long main street is overlooked by the Cathedral of St Eunan, built around 100 years ago and containing some important stained glass. The Donegal County Museum has artefacts from the Stone Age to medieval periods as well as more recent history and folk life. In Church Hill, on the shore of Lough Gartan, the lovely **Glebe House** is an art gallery, and just outside the town on the Glenties road is the Newmills Corn & Flax Mills.

74B3

Glebe House and Gallery

✉ Churchill

☎ 074-9137071

Easter & mid-May to late Sep 11–6:30. Closed Fri

Tea room (£)

Few; ground floor only

Cheap

Londonderry's Victorian Guildhall towers over Shipquay Street

⊞ 74B3

Tower Museum
✉ Union Hall Place
☎ 028 7137 2411
🕐 Jul–Aug daily 10–4:30;
   Mar–Jun Mon–Sat
   10–4:30; rest of year
   Mon–Fri 10–4:30
🚻 Londonderry
♿ Good
💷 Moderate

LONDONDERRY   ✪✪

Londonderry is a city that is historically absorbing, yet lively and modern too, with lots of festivals, events and enter-tainments. The perfect introduction is to take a guided walk of about 1.5km around its 17th-century town walls, which are still unbroken in spite of a 105-day siege by Jacobite forces in 1689, one of the most significant battles in Irish history. The city had hardly ever been trouble-free. Ever since St Columba founded his first monastery here in AD 546, its strategic and accessible location on the Foyle estuary attracted marauders. You can learn more of the history of the town at the **Tower Museum**.

> ### *Did you know ?*
>
> *The English forces, who took the city of Derry in the mid-16th century, accidentally blew up most of the medieval city when their munitions exploded. The subsequent rebuilding was carried out (somewhat unwillingly) by the City of London Guilds, hence the 'London' prefix. To this day many people still adhere to the city's original name of Derry.*

Londonderry has impressive public buildings, two fine cathedrals and dramatic townscapes, but there are also lots of little lanes to explore, and behind the 19th-century Guildhall is the quay from which so many emigrants sailed for the New World.

LOUGH NEAGH   ✪

⊞ 75C2

Lough Neagh, the largest lake in the British Isles, has little hidden harbours, sandy beaches and a number of islands.

Lakes are always best explored by boat, and Lough Neagh is no exception, because the roads around it rarely follow the waterline. The *Irish Mist* cruises around the lake from the marina at Antrim, a busy and attractive town, with a famous 9th-century round tower.

In the southeastern corner of the lough, Oxford Island has a range of habitats for birdlife, including wet meadows, reedbeds, woodlands and shoreline scrub. The **Lough Neagh Discovery Centre** here has audio-visual shows and interactive games, and visitors can participate in guided walks or take a boat trip.

For more seclusion, there are hides for birdwatching and a variety of marked walking trails.

THE MOUNTAINS OF MOURNE ✪✪

Percy French wrote many popular songs extolling the beauty of Ireland, but his best-known line must surely be *'where the Mountains of Mourne sweep down to the sea'*. Few first-time visitors, though, would be prepared for the wild beauty of the scenery.

The **Mourne Heritage Trust** at Newcastle is a good place to start, with lots of information and guided walks. One of the nature trails follows the 'Brandy Pad', a notorious smugglers' route that links Hilltown, appropriately notable for its many pubs, with the coast south of Newcastle.

Slieve Donard, at 839m, is the highest mountain, and clothing its slopes is the Donard Forest Park. There is more woodland in the Tollymore and Castlewellan forest parks, while to the south is the evocatively named Silent Valley, flooded to form two great reservoirs. There is a charge for cars to enter the forest parks and Silent Valley, which are accessible from about 10AM (closing time varies depending on the season).

Lough Neagh Discovery Centre

✉ Oxford Island

☎ 028 3832 2205

🕐 Apr–Sep daily 10–6 (until 7 Sun); Oct–Mar Mon–Sun 10–5

🍴 Cafe (££)

♿ Good

🚻 Moderate

➕ 75D1

Mourne Heritage Trust

✉ 87 Central Promenade, Newcastle

☎ 028 4372 4059; www.mournealive.com

🕐 Mon–Fri 9–5

♿ Good

🚻 Free

Newcastle nestles beneath the beautiful Mountains of Mourne

MOUNT STEWART HOUSE AND GARDENS ●●●

One of Ireland's grandest stately homes, Mount Stewart was built for the 3rd Marquess of Londonderry. Three architects were involved in the building – James Wyatt, in the 1780s, then George Dance and (probably) William Vitruvious Morrison in the early 19th century. The imposing interior largely reflects the impeccable taste of the 7th Marchioness, a leader of London society in the 1920s and 1930s. She was also responsible for the beautiful garden, among the very best in the care of the National Trust, which benefits from the mild climate between the Irish Sea and Strangford Lough.

ULSTER-AMERICAN FOLK PARK (▶ 26, TOP TEN)

ULSTER FOLK AND TRANSPORT MUSEUM ●●

All kinds of Ulster buildings have been painstakingly dismantled in their original locations, brought to this 25-hectare site and reconstructed in authentic settings, including a small town of the 1900s, complete with shops, a school, churches, printer's workshops, a bank and terraced houses. Rural exhibits include traditional Irish cottages, watermills and farmhouses, and farming is represented by rare breeds of animals and fields which are cultivated using traditional methods.

The Transport Museum is very comprehensive, covering all forms of transport from horse-drawn carts to the De Lorean car, and includes the superb Irish Railway Collection and The Flight Experience, an interactive exhibition.

Mount Stewart House and Gardens

- ✚ 75D2
- ✉ 8km southeast of Newtownards
- ☎ 028 4278 8387
- 🕐 Grounds: May–Sep daily 10–8; Apr, Oct 10–6; Nov–Mar 10–4. House: Jul–Aug daily 12–6; May–Jun, Sep Mon, Wed–Fri 1–6, Sat–Sun 12–6; mid-Mar to Apr, Oct Sat–Sun & public hols 12–6
- 🚌 Ulsterbus 9 & 10 from Belfast–Portaferry
- 🚲 Bangor
- ♿ Few 🏷 Moderate

Ulster Folk and Transport Museum

- ✚ 75D2
- ✉ Bangor Road, Cultra, Holywood
- ☎ 028 9042 8428; www.uftm.org.uk
- 🕐 Mar–Jun Mon–Sat 10–6, Sun 11–6; Jul–Sep Mon–Sat 10–6, Sun 11–6; Oct–Feb Mon–Fri 10–4, Sat 10–5, Sun 11–5
- 🍴 Tea room (£)
- 🚌 B1,B2 from Belfast to Bangor
- 🚲 Cultra Halt
- ♿ Very good 🏷 Moderate

Perennially popular is the *Titanic* exhibition, on the 'unsinkable' liner which was built in Belfast's shipyards and foundered after hitting an iceberg on her maiden voyage.

As well as the permanent exhibitions, the museum has special events, which change from year to year.

Opposite: *Mount Stewart House and gardens*
Below: *a fine old kitchen at the Ulster Folk Museum*

WELLBROOK BEETLING MILL

This water-powered 18th-century linen hammer mill is a testament to the history of linen making in Northern Ireland. For much of the 19th century the north of Ireland was the world's greatest producer of linen and you can see demonstrations of how the material was made. Tours are conducted around the mill and costumed interpreters will explain the process of manufacture and you can try your hand at scutching, hackling, weaving and beetling. Beetling is the final process in linen manufacture when the cloth is repeatedly hammered to prodce a sheen – the heavy hammers used were known as beetles. The process could last for anything between two days and two weeks. The mill's seven water-powered beetling engines create a thunderous noise and it is said that it was not unusual for the beetlers to become completely or partial deaf working in a confined space for up to 15 hours a day.

The mill is set in a lovely wooded glen on the banks of the fast-flowing River Ballinderry – complete with salmon and brown trout – and there are a number of pleasant riverside walks and places to have a picnic.

74B2
Wellbrook Road, Corkhill (6.5km west of Cookstown)
028 8674 8210
Mid–Mar to Jun & Sep Sat–Sun 11–6; Jul–Aug daily 11–6
Ulsterbus 90 from Cookstown, request stop at Kildress then 1km walk
Good
Moderate
Shop; scenic walks

The Spectacular Antrim Coast

Distance
160km

Time
About 7 hours

Start/end point
Larne
➕ 75D3

Lunch
Wysner's (£)
✉ 16 Ann Street,
Ballycastle
☎ 028 2076 2372

From Larne take the A2 north signed Glenarm and the Antrim Coast Road.

All the way to Ballycastle there is wonderful coastal scenery and pretty villages. Turn off to explore the Glens of Antrim if you have time.

Pass Bonamargy Friary on the left and at the T-junction turn left into Ballycastle. From the Diamond take the A2 signposted 'Portrush, Bushmills, Giant's Causeway'. Soon turn right, signposted 'Ballintoy, B15, Coastal Route'. At the T-junction turn right and continue, passing the turning to Carrick-a-Rede Rope Bridge.

In summer the rope bridge is strung high above the water across the gap between the mainland and a little rocky island.

Go through Ballintoy and after 5.6km turn right into Causeway Road. After another 5.6km you reach the Visitor Centre.

This is a World Heritage Site and a unique phenomenon which should not be missed.

Spectacular scenery at Glenarm on the Antrim Coast Road

From the Causeway, take the A2 to Bushmills and at the roundabout in the village go straight on, signposted 'Dervock'. After a short distance, reach the Bushmills Distillery on the left.

Though it is a large-scale working distillery, Bushmills is well geared up for visitors, with an interesting and entertaining tour, tastings and shops.

Continue to Dervock, then at T-junction turn right with the B66, signposted 'Ballymoney'. About 6.4km farther on turn left on to the A26. Keep on this road and at the end of its short motorway section, reach a roundabout and turn left on to A36. Follow signs back to Larne.

Where To...

Above: *Folk music at
Bailey's Corner, Tralee*
Right: *Kilkenny pub sign*

The East

Prices
The following symbols indicate the approximate prices for a three-course meal for one person:

€ = under €25
€€ = €25–€45
€€€ = over €45

for Northern Ireland
£ = under £15
££ = £15–£30
£££ = over £30

Black and White
Guinness developed from an 18th-century beer called porter because it was brewed for the porters in London's Billingsgate market. The drink was brought to Ireland by Cork brewers, Beamish and Crawford, and became known as stout when Guinness increased its alcoholic content and sold it as 'extra stout porter'.

Dalkey
Co Dublin
Guinea Pig (The Fish Restaurant) (€€€)
Family-run restaurant, adorned with rustic brass ornaments and decorative plates, with an extensive, though not exclusively, seafood-based menu.
✉ 17 Railway Road, Dalkey ☎ 01-2859055 🕒 Dinner only

Dublin
Co Dublin
Dublin has an enormous variety of places to eat and drink, with every kind of international food available. For lively and entertaining café-bars and cosmopolitan restaurants, head for Temple Bar; for more elegance and sophistication, look along Baggot Street and around Ballsbridge.

Il Baccaro (€€)
An intimate Italian restaurant set in a lovely 17th-century cellar in the heart of Temple Bar.
✉ Diceman's Corner, Meeting House Square ☎ 01-6714597 🕒 Lunch (Fri–Sun), dinner

Café Mao (€€)
Fashionable eaterie with a slick interior serving delicious stir fries and oriental dishes such as Malaysian chicken.
✉ 2–3 Chatham Row ☎ 01-6704899 🕒 Lunch, dinner

Kelly & Ping (€€)
A blend of Irish (the bar) and Far Eastern (the food) in the northside's new cultural heartland. Extensive menu of interesting dishes.
✉ Smithfield Village ☎ 01-8173840 🕒 Lunch and dinner Mon–Fri, Sat dinner only

Oliver St John Gogarty (€–€€)
Historic, atmospheric pub in the heart of Temple Bar with pub food downstairs and a restaurant on the top floor. Excellent seafood, organic ingredients and vegetarian choices. Traditional music most days.
✉ 58-59 Fleet Street, Temple Bar ☎ 01-6711822 🕒 Lunch, dinner (Sun dinner only)

Patrick Guilbaud (€€€)
Right up there among Dublin's finest restaurants. French cuisine.
✉ Merion Hotel, 21 Upper Merrion Street ☎ 01-6764192 🕒 Lunch, dinner. Closed Sun & Mon

Queen of Tarts (€)
Super homemade cakes and pastries. Salads and cream teas, too. All served in initimate surroundings by friendly staff.
✉ 4 Cork Hill, Dame Street ☎ 01-6707499 🕒 Daily

Thai Orchid (€€)
Delicious Thai food and courteous service from Thai staff in traditional costume.
✉ 7 Westmoreland Street ☎ 01-6719969 🕒 Lunch Mon–Fri; dinner daily

Enniskerry
Co Wicklow
Powerscourt Terrace Café (€)
Wonderful views over the Powerscourt gardens and to the mountains beyond.
✉ Powerscourt House ☎ 01-2046070 🕒 Lunch only

Glencullen
Co Dublin
Johnnie Foxes Pub (€)

An 18th-century coaching inn, complete with beams and open fires, known for its excellent seafood, with fresh mussels a speciality. Music and dancing nightly.

✉ **Dublin Mountains** ☎ 01-2955647 🕔 Lunch, dinner. Closed Sun lunch, Good Fri & 25 Dec

Greystones
Co Wicklow
Hungry Monk (€€)

The place for a romantic candlelit supper overlooking a scenic golf course. Good traditional Irish dishes.

✉ **Church Road** ☎ 01-2875759 🕔 Dinner Wed–Sat, lunch Sun only

Howth
Co Dublin
King Sitric Fish Restaurant (€€€)

Famous fish restaurant, which has won many awards.

✉ **East Pier** ☎ 01-8325235 🕔 Lunch Mon–Fri, dinner Mon–Sat. Closed Sun

Kildare
Co Kildare
Silken Thomas (€–€€)

Victorian-style restaurant and bars in the centre of town with an international menu.

✉ **The Square** ☎ 045-521264 🕔 Lunch, dinner

Kilkenny
Co Kilkenny
Kilkenny Design Centre (€)

The restaurant at this complex of craft workshops matches up to the quality Irish craft wares on sale. Traditional Irish dishes and vegetarian selections.

✉ **Castle Yard** ☎ 056-7722118 🕔 Daily during shopping hours

Kilmacanoge
Co Wicklow
Avoca Handweavers (€)

Set in the Wicklow Mountains, you'll find delicious home-cooked food. Caters well for vegetarians.

✉ **Kilmacanoge** ☎ 01-2867466 🕔 Mon–Sat 9:30–5:30, Sun 10–6

Leighlinbridge
Co Carlow
The Lord Bagenal Inn (€€)

Beside the River Barrow, this award winning pub serves international and Irish cuisine, including seafood. Accommodation.

✉ **Main Street** ☎ 059-9721668 🕔 Lunch, dinner 12–6. Bar meals Mon–Sat 9AM–10PM, Sun 9AM–9PM

Malahide
Co Dublin
Bon Appetit (€€€)

There is a first-class wine list to accompany the international menu with seafood specialities.

✉ **9 James Terrace** ☎ 01-8450314 🕔 Lunch, dinner. Closed Sun & public hols, Sat lunch

Roundwood
Co Wicklow
Roundwood Inn (€€)

Cosy pub offering seafood, game and traditional Irish dishes.

✉ **Roundwood** ☎ 01-2818107 🕔 Restaurant: lunch Sun only, dinner Fri–Sun. Pub food daily, all day

Wexford
Co Wexford
The Wrens Nest (€)

A great place to meet the locals. Good bar meals.

✉ **Custom House Quay** ☎ 053-22359 🕔 Lunch Mon–Sat

Famous Drinkers
Ireland's famous writers were also great drinkers and had their favourites among Dublin's old pubs. A literary pub crawl takes you around the most famous of them, with professional actors performing from the works of Joyce, O'Casey, Yeats, Behan et al. Tickets are available from the tourist office.

The South

Floating Food
Cruising restaurants ply the waters of the rivers Barrow and Nore from New Ross and Waterford, offering a wonderfully relaxing way to eat and enjoy the scenery at the same time. The *St Ciaran* and the *St Brendan* can carry 70 or 80 diners. Lunch, afternoon tea and dinner cruises are all available, April to October. Booking is essential.

The Galley Cruising Restaurant (€€€)
✉ The Quay, New Ross
☎ 051-421723;
www.rivercruise.ie
🕐 Apr–end Oct

Adrigole
Co Cork
Mossie's (€–€€)
Charming restaurant housed in former presbytery with sunroom and terraces overlooking Bantry Bay. Also operates as a B&B.
✉ Ulsker House ☎ 027-60606 🕐 Lunch, dinner Tue–Sun May–Sep; dinner Thu–Sat, and Sun lunch, Oct–Apr

Adare
Co Limerick
Dunraven Arms (€–€€€)
Delightful country inn with an award-winning restaurant.
☎ 061-396633 🕐 Lunch Sun only, dinner daily

Ballingarry
Co Limerick
The Mustard Seed (€€€)
A pleasant drive through the Limerick countryside on quiet lanes leads to this first-class restaurant in a stylish country house. Also B&B.
✉ Echo Lodge ☎ 069-68508 🕐 Dinner only. Closed 24–26 Dec

Baltimore
Co Cork
Chez Youen (€€–€€€)
This is among the best fish restaurants in Ireland. It's worth driving up to the Beacon afterwards for views over the bay.
✉ The Square ☎ 028-20136 🕐 Lunch Sun only, dinner daily in summer, Thu–Sat in winter

La Jolie Brise (€–€€)
This cheerful pizzeria, under the same management as Chez Youen, also offers a selection of fish and steak dishes.
✉ The Square ☎ 028-20600 🕐 All year, all day

Bantry
Co Cork
O'Connor's Seafood Restaurant (€–€€)
Fresh local fish and shellfish are the specialities here.
✉ The Square ☎ 027-50221 🕐 Lunch, dinner

Cloghroe
Co Cork
Blairs Inn (€–€€)
In a secluded riverside setting near Blarney. Good Irish cuisine, including fish, duck, steaks and game all from local sources. Traditional music Mondays in summer.
✉ Cloghroe, Blarney ☎ 021-4381470 🕐 Lunch, dinner & all-day bar menu

Cork
Co Cork
Crawford Art Gallery (€€)
Excellent Irish and Mediterranean dishes.
✉ Emmet Place ☎ 021-4274415 🕐 Breakfast, lunch & afternoon tea. Closed Sun

Jacques (€€)
Well-reviewed restaurant creating modern Irish dishes from excellent local produce, including farm-reared ducks, fish and organic vegetables.
✉ Phoenix Street ☎ 021-4277387 🕐 Lunch Mon–Fri, dinner Mon–Sat

Dingle
Co Kerry
The Charthouse (€–€€)
Award-winning chefs and cuisine in this cosy harbour-side restaurant.
✉ The Mail Road ☎ 066-9152255 🕐 Dinner daily Mar–Oct; Thu–Sun Nov–Feb

Lord Baker's (€€)
Fish, game and succulent

steaks are the speciality of
this award-winning restaurant.
📧 Main Street ☎ 066-
9151277 🕐 Lunch, dinner.
Closed Thu & 24–6 Dec

Dunmore East
Co Waterford
The Ship (€€)
Wonderful fresh lobster and
prawns, French and Irish
dishes are served in this
charming pub.
☎ 051-383141 🕐 Dinner
daily Apr–Oct; Wed–Sat,
Oct–Mar. Lunch daily Jul–Aug;
Sun all year

Kenmare
Co Kerry
Prego (€–€€)
Good atmosphere and tasty
food in this well-priced family
restaurant.
📧 Henry Street ☎ 064-42350
🕐 Lunch and dinner daily.
Closed 25–26 Dec

Packie's (€€)
Stylish but unpretentious
restaurant with creative
cooking; intensely flavoured
Irish-Mediterranean food.
📧 Henry Street ☎ 064-41508
🕐 Dinner Tue–Sat mid-Mar to
mid Oct (Jun–Aug Mon–Sat); Oct
to mid-Jan Wed–Sat

Killarney
Co Kerry
Foley's Seafood and Steak
Restaurant (€€)
The name says it all, and the
restaurant is famous for it.
📧 23 High Street ☎ 064-
31217 🕐 Lunch, dinner. Closed
24–6 Dec & lunch in winter

Old Presbytery Restaurant
(€€)
Quality Irish ingredients are
well prepared in this
attractive Georgian
restaurant.

📧 Cathedral Place
☎ 064-30555 🕐 Lunch,
dinner Wed–Mon. Closed Jan
and Tue

Kinsale
Co Cork
Fishy Fishy (€)
Fresh fish, shellfish, salads
and desserts feature at this
popular restaurant.
📧 Market Palce ☎ 021-
4774453 🕐 Daily 10–4. Closed
Sun Oct–Mar

Man Friday (€€)
One of Kinsale's longest-
established restaurants, Man
Friday has an excellent
reputation and awards for its
modern Irish and
international cuisine.
📧 Scilly ☎ 021-4772260
🕐 Dinner only. Closed Sun
(except bank hol Sun)

Limerick
Co Limerick
Duckarts (€)
This museum restaurant
serves good food and has
lovely Shannon side views.
📧 Hunt Museum, The Custom
House, Rutland Street ☎ 061-
312833 🕐 Mon–Sat 10–5,
Sun 2–5

Freddy's Bistro (€€)
This restaurant, serving a
range of Irish and continental
dishes, is full of character.
📧 Theatre Lane, Lower
Glentworth Street ☎ 061-
418749 🕐 Dinner Tue–Sat

Waterford
Co Waterford
The Wine Vault
(€–€€)
A warm and cosy wine bar
specialising in seafood.
📧 High Street ☎ 051-853444
🕐 Lunch, dinner. Closed Sun,
Good Fri & 25 Dec

Courses for Cooks
Surrounded by the lush
countryside of Co Cork,
the Ballymaloe Cookery
School is internationally
renowned. It offers a
range of courses for all
abilities, from novices to
professionals, from a
single day to a 12-week
course, and the school's
own kitchen gardens
provide superb ingredients
to work with. The school is
run by Darina Allen, who
has created a lovely
informal atmosphere.

The West

Oysters

One of the most popular images of Irish cuisine is a plate of oysters and a pint of Guinness, and there is nowhere better to sample the two together than at the Galway International Oyster Festival in September. Oysters are only eaten when there is an 'r' in the month, so this festival marks the beginning of the season and is a wonderful gastronomic celebration, accompanied by non-stop entertainment.

Aran Islands
Co Galway

Mainistir House (€€)

Come here for a quirky dining experience overlooking the bay. Daily changing set menu.

✉ Inis Mór (Inishmore) ☎ 099-61169; www.mainistirhouse.com

🕓 Dinner daily at 8PM

Ballyvaughan
Co Clare

Hyland's Burren Hotel (€–€€)

Located close to the harbour, the hotel offers an excellent range of dishes. There is a popular bar menu for lunches. Good accommodation, too.

✉ Ballyvaughan ☎ 065-7077037; www.hylandsburren.com 🕓 Lunch, dinner. Closed Jan–Feb

Monks Bar & Restaurant (€)

Renowned for its seafood chowder, Monks is a seafood speciality restaurant overlooking Galway Bay.

☎ 065-7077059 🕓 Lunch, dinner

Clarenbridge
Co Galway

Paddy Burke's (€–€€)

Famous as the focal point of the Clarenbridge Oyster Festival; no prizes for guessing the speciality dish.

☎ 091-796226; www.paddyburkesgalway.com 🕓 Lunch, dinner. Closed Good Fri & 25 Dec

Clifden
Co Galway

Mitchell's (€€)

Hearty Irish stew is the speciality here, with good portions of seafood and steaks from a varied menu.

✉ Market Street ☎ 095-21867 🕓 Lunch, dinner. Closed mid-Nov to mid-Mar

Collooney
Co Sligo

Markree Castle (€€€)

You can enjoy seafood, game and European dishes in magnificent surroundings at this historic castle hotel.

☎ 071-9167800; www.markreecastle.ie 🕓 Breakfast, daily lunch, dinner

Foxford
Co Mayo

Lough Cullin Room Restaurant (€€)

Fish and game speciality menu in this charming restaurant overlooking Lough Cullin.

✉ Healy's Hotel, Pontoon ☎ 094-9256443 🕓 Dinner

Galway
Co Galway

Huntsman Inn (€–€€)

Renovated building with a cosy interior and good-value, and quality bar food.

✉ College Road ☎ 091-562849 🕓 Daily noon–9

Kirbys of Cross Street (€–€€)

Good value contemporary cuisine on Irish themes, seasoned with influences from further afield.

✉ Cross Street ☎ 091-569404 🕓 Lunch, dinner

Kirwan's Lane Restaurant (€€–€€€)

Stylish modern restaurant serving bistro-style grills and Asian influenced dishes.

✉ Kirwan's Lane ☎ 091-568266 🕓 Lunch and dinner Mon–Sat, dinner only Sun. Closed 25 Dec

Trattoria Pasta Mista (€–€€)
Fresh homemade pasta and traditional Italian dishes in the heart of the city.
✉ 12 Quay Street ☎ 091-563910 🕐 Lunch, dinner

Tulsi Restaurant (€)
Award-winning restaurant with tandoori specialities, biryani dishes, plus seafood and vegetarian options.
✉ Buttermilk Walk, Middle Street ☎ 091-569518 🕐 Lunch, dinner

Kilcolgan
Co Galway
Morans Oyster Cottage (€–€€€)
Famous for its seafood. Specialities include chowder and smoked salmon.
✉ The Weir ☎ 091-796113 🕐 Lunch, dinner

Lisdoonvarna
Co Clare
Sheedy's Country House Hotel (€€–€€€)
Set in lovely gardens, this family-run hotel-restaurant has won awards for food and hospitality.
✉ Sheedy's Spa View Hotel ☎ 065-7074026 🕐 Lunch (bar meals), dinner. Closed mid-Oct to Easter

Moycullen
Co Galway
White Gables Restaurant (€€–€€€)
This charming restaurant has a high reputation for its French cuisine and seafood.
☎ 091-555744 🕐 Dinner Mon–Sat; lunch Sun only. Closed 23 Dec to mid-Feb

Recess
Co Galway
Ballynahinch Castle
(€€–€€€)
Local game, fish and fresh produce inspire the menus.
✉ On Roundstone road, off N59, 5km west of Recess ☎ 095-31006 🕐 Lunch (bar meals), dinner. Closed 29 Jan–23 Feb and 15–27 Dec

Roundstone
Co Galway
O'Dowd's Seafood (€€)
Traditional pub with restaurant serving excellent Irish cooking and local fish.
☎ 095-35809; www.odowdsrestaurant.com 🕐 Lunch, dinner

Sligo
Co Sligo
Embassy Rooms and The Belfry (€–€€)
Right in the heart of the town, this large restaurant has won awards for both its à la carte and its bar food.
✉ John F Kennedy Parade ☎ 071-9161250 🕐 Lunch, dinner. Closed Good Fri, 25 Dec

Fiddler's Creek (€€–€€€)
Good wholesome steak and fish dishes.
✉ Rockwood Parade ☎ 071-914 1866 🕐 Dinner daily, lunch Sun only

Westport
Co Mayo
Asgard Bar and Restaurant (€€–€€€)
Overlooking Clew Bay; good seafood and Irish specialities.
✉ The Quay ☎ 098-25319 🕐 Lunch, dinner. Closed Mon & Tue off season

Quay Cottage (€€)
Local shellfish and seafood are the speciality here.
✉ The Harbour ☎ 098-26412 🕐 Dinner only. Closed Christmas, mid-Jan to mid-Feb

Banquets
Irish medieval banquets are great fun, even if they are blatantly aimed at the tourist trade. Bunratty and Knappogue castles are the most popular venues for these evenings of feasting in an authentic setting, with staff in medieval costume and traditional music.

The North

Afternoon Tea
National Trust tea rooms
are well known for the
quality of their cakes and
scones, and those in
Northern Ireland have the
added benefit of the Ulster
tradition of home-baking.
Recipes include an
amazing variety of breads,
potato cakes, soda breads,
barm brack and biscuits.
Rounding off a visit to one
of the magnificent stately
homes with afternoon tea
is a real treat.

Throughout the Province of
Northern Ireland look out for
the green and white 'Taste
of Ulster' sign, which
guarantees the best of fresh,
local produce.

Annalong
Co Down
**Glassdrumman Lodge
(£££)**
Prime local produce,
including prawns and
salmon, feature on the six-
course dinner menu of well-
produced dishes.
✉ 85 Mill Road ☎ 028 4376
8451 🕐 Dinner; bookings
essential

Ballycastle
Co Antrim
Wysner's (£–££)
Pleasant two-storey
restaurant in the centre of
town, with reasonably priced
dishes, including traditional
Irish and a good selection of
healthy eating options.
✉ 16 Ann Street ☎ 028 2076
2372 🕐 Lunch, dinner. Closed
Sun

Ballymena
Co Antrim
**Galgorm Resort and Spa
(££–£££)**
The restaurant of this
restored 19th-century
mansion offers fine dining
overlooking the River Maine.
✉ 136 Fenaghy Road ☎ 028
2588 1001 🕐 Lunch, dinner

Bangor
Co Down
Clandeboye Lodge Hotel (£)
Interesting treatment of
good local produce in a
secluded location.
✉ 10 Estate Road, Clandeboye
☎ 028 9185 2500 🕐 Lunch,
dinner, bar food. Closed
24–6 Dec

Belfast
In Belfast, the 'Golden Mile'
between the Grand Opera
House and Queen's
University is the best place
to search out good
restaurants. The city-centre
shopping areas also have
no shortage of coffee shops,
fast food outlets and
atmospheric pubs.

Morning Star (££)
A historic Belfast pub with
exceptionally good food,
using only the freshest
Ulster produce and seafood.
✉ 17 Pottinger's Entry ☎ 028
9032 3976 🕐 Lunch daily,
dinner Mon–Sat

Nick's Warehouse (££)
A modern restaurant set in a
converted warehouse. Nick
Price's excellent cooking has
justifiably attracted praise.
✉ 35 Hill Street ☎ 028 9043
9690 🕐 Lunch Mon–Fri, dinner
Mon–Sat

The Northern Wing (£–££)
Caesar salad, beef and
Guinness sausages, salmon
goujons and more served in
this in this old printing press
now restored into a stylish
restaurant.
✉ 2 Bridge Street ☎ 028
9050 9888 🕐 All day menu

Olio (£)
Warm and welcoming
restaurant offering a range of
European and Cajun dishes.
✉ 17 Brunswick Street
☎ 028 9024 0239 🕐 noon–
10PM (11 Fri, Sat). Closed Sun

**Restaurant Michael Deane
(£££)**
Perfect fusion food is cooked
in full view of his customers
by celebrity chef Michael
Deane.

✉ **34–40 Howard Street**
☎ 028 9033 1134;
www.michaeldeane.co.uk
🕔 Dinner Wed–Sat

Shu (££–£££)
Cosmopolitan brasserie-style
restaurant which has
received many accolades
since opening in 2000.
✉ **252 Lisburn Road**
☎ 028 9038 1655;
www.shu-restaurant.com
🕔 Lunch, dinner. Closed Sun

Donegal
Co Donegal
Harbour Restaurant (€–€€)
A cosy restaurant offering a
good variety of international
and Irish dishes.
✉ **Quay Street** ☎ 074-
9721702 🕔 Lunch Sun,
dinner daily

Enniskillen
Co Fermanagh
Killyhevlin Hotel (£–££)
Excellent food and wonderful
views over Lough Erne.
✉ **Dublin Road, Killyhevlin**
☎ 028 6632 3481
🕔 Breakfast, lunch, dinner

Hillsborough
Co Down
**Hillside Restaurant and Bar
(££)**
Traditional country-house
cooking with global
influences in this award-
winning pub.
✉ **21 Main Street** ☎ 028
9268 2765 🕔 Bar: lunch,
dinner. Restaurant: dinner Fri,
Sat. Closed evenings Good Fri &
25 Dec

Killyleagh
Co Down
Dufferin Arms (£–££)
European, seafood and
vegetarian choices feature
heavily on the menu at this

well-known country pub.
✉ **35 High Street**
☎ 028 4482 1182
🕔 Lunch, dinner

Limavady
Co Londonderry
The Lime Tree (££)
Modern Irish cuisine using
the best of seasonal local
produce.
✉ **60 Catherine Street** ☎ 028
7776 4300 🕔 Dinner only
Tue–Sat. Closed 25–26 Dec

Londonderry
Co Londonderry
**Beech Hill Country House
Hotel (££–£££)**
This exclusive hotel in a
peaceful location has an
excellent award-winning
restaurant.
✉ **32 Ardmore Road** ☎ 028
7134 9279; www.beech-hill.com
🕔 Breakfast, lunch, dinner.
Closed 25 Dec

Omagh
Co Tyrone
Mellon Country Inn (££)
The Mellon serves up
traditional Irish cuisine with a
modern twist.
✉ **134 Beltany Road**
☎ 028 8166 1224 🕔 Lunch,
dinner

Portaferry
Co Down
Portaferry Hotel (£££)
A charming 18th-century inn
picturesquely set on the
edge of Strangford Lough.
The restaurant is best known
for its seafood.
✉ **10 The Strand**
☎ 028 4272 8231
🕔 Lunch, early evening menu,
à la carte dinner. Closed
24–5 Dec

Themed Foods
Special events at the
Ulster-American Folk Park
near Omagh usually offer
the chance to taste some
kind of traditional
delicacies, either of the
Old Country or the New
World. At the Frontier
Festival Weekends in
summer, guests can enjoy
pioneer cooking, while at
the end of October
Halloween fare
accompanies the dramatic
antics around the park.

The East

Prices

The symbol indicates an approximate price for two people sharing a double room

€ = under €100
€€ = €100–€200
€€€ = over €200

for Northern Ireland

£ = under £70
££ = £70–£130
£££ = over £130

Avoca
Co Wicklow
Sheepwalk House (€)

A cosy 18th-century house 3km from Avoca with lovely views over the Arklow Valley.

✉ Beech Road, Avoca
☎ 0402-35189;
www.sheepwalk.com
◉ Closed Dec–Jan

Dublin
Charleville Lodge (€–€€)

This highly recommended guesthouse is in a Victorian terrace near Phoenix Park.

✉ 268–272 North Circular Road
☎ 01-8386633;
www.charlevillelodge.ie
◉ Closed 21–26 Dec

Chief O'Neill's (€€€)

In revitalised Smithfield Village, this luxurious hotel is dedicated to the memory of Francis O'Neill, Chicago chief of police and collector of Irish traditional music.

✉ Smithfield Village
☎ 01-8173838;
www.chiefoneills.com

Harding (€)

Good value hotel close to Temple Bar and opposite Christ Church Cathedral. Bright, cheerful furnishings and ensuite bathrooms. Bar and restaurant with music some evenings. Helpful, friendly staff.

✉ Copper Alley, Fishamble Street ☎ 01-6796500;
www.hardinghotel.ie

Kilronian House (€€)

This stylish Georgian house is in a peaceful location close to the National Concert Hall.

✉ 70 Adelaide Road
☎ 01-475 5266;
www.dublinn.com

Merrion (€€€)

The epitome of relaxed grandeur, the Merrion, formerly four gracious townhouses, has superb bedrooms and opulent bathrooms that reflect the 18th-century architecture.

✉ Upper Merrion Street
☎ 01-6030600;
www.merrionhotel.com

Kilkenny
Co Kilkenny
Butler House (€€–€€€)

Georgian mansion with elegant interiors, restored by the Irish State Design Agency. Peaceful location, but close enough to the city centre and castle to be a good base for sightseeing.

✉ 16 Patrick Street ☎ 056-7765707; www.butler.ie
◉ Closed 24–9 Dec

Rathnew
Co Wicklow
Hunters Hotel (€€)

Rambling 16th-century coaching inn has loads of character and lovely gardens running down to the river. Good restaurant featuring some excellent fish dishes.

✉ Newrath Bridge ☎ 0404-40106; www.hunters.ie

Tinakilly Country House (€€–€€€)

Elegant mansion is set in 3ha of grounds, with sea views.

☎ 0404-69274; www.tinakilly.ie

Straffan
Co Kildare
Kildare Hotel and Country Club (€€€)

Sheer luxury and excellent food in magnificent surroundings. Facilities include a golf course and private fishing.

☎ 01-6017200; www.kclub.ie

The South

Adare
Co Limerick
Adare Manor (€€€)
An opulent hotel in a Gothic mansion, surrounded by 340ha of parkland beside the River Maigue; including a championship golf course and other leisure facilities.
✉ On Limerick to Tralee route
☎ 061-396566; www.adare manor.com

Ballylickey
Co Cork
Sea View House (€€)
A delightful country-house hotel overlooking Bantry Bay.
☎ 027-50073;
www.seaviewhousehotel.com
🕐 Closed mid-Nov to mid-Mar

Clonakilty
Co Cork
Inchydoney Island Lodge & Spa (€€€)
Award-winning hotel in a blue flag beach setting. Home to Ireland's only thalassotherapy spa.
✉ Clonakilty ☎ 023-33143;
www.inchydoneyisland.com

Cork
Co Cork
Isaacs Hotel (€€)
One of Cork's finest hotels with good accommodation and the celebrated Greenes Restaurant.
✉ 48 MacCurtain Street
☎ 021-4503805; www.isaccs.ie

Kenmare
Co Kerry
Brooklane Hotel (€–€€)
This new hotel offers friendly, personal service. Casey's restaurant has good food and Irish music and the Cinnamon Club hosts top Irish music artists.
✉ Gortamullen ☎ 064-42077;
www.brooklanehotel.com

Park Hotel (€€€)
Country house hotel by Kenmare Bay and home to the deluxe spa 'Samas'.
✉ On the R569 ☎ 064-41200;
www.parkkenmare.com
🕐 Closed 4 Jan–10 Apr

Killarney
Co Kerry
Aghadoe Heights (€€€)
Situated high above the Killarney Lakes, this hotel offers luxury and hospitality and a great restaurant.
✉ 5km north of Killarney off N22 Tralee road ☎ 064-31766;
www.aghadoeheights.com
🕐 Check for winter closure

Kinsale
Co Cork
Deasy's Long Quay House (€€)
Splendid Georgian residence overlooking the inner harbour and yacht marina.
✉ Long Quay ☎ 021-4774563;
www.longquayhousekinsale.com 🕐 Closed Nov, Dec

Limerick
Co Limerick
Best Western Pery's Hotel (€€)
Historic city centre hotel located right in the heart of Georgian Limerick.
✉ Glentworth Street
☎ 061-413822; www.perys.ie

Waterford
Co Waterford
Waterford Castle & Golf Club (€€€)
A castle on an island with many of its original features, including 16th-century oak panelling and stone walls. Modern leisure facilities and an 18-hole golf course.
✉ The Island, Ballinakill
☎ 051-878203;
www.waterfordcastle.com

Sporting Activities
Many visitors to Ireland come specifically to indulge in one of three sporting activities – angling, golf and horse-riding. Hotels, guest houses and self-catering establishments have been quick to recognise the demand, and a large number of them will make all the necessary arrangements for their guests to enjoy their chosen activity.

The West

Irish Kings

Clonalis House in Co Roscommon is the home of the O'Conors of Connacht, descendants of the Kings of Connacht and the last High King of Ireland. It was built in Victorian times on land owned by the family for 1,500 years.

Guests here can browse through old family manuscripts and see the harp which belonged to the great Turlough O'Carolan.

Clonalis House (€€)
✉ On the west side of Castlerea on the N60
☎ 9496-20014
🕐 Closed Oct to mid-Apr

Ballynahinch
Co Galway

Ballynahinch Castle (€€€)
Furnished with antiques, Ballynahinch Castle offers high standards of food and accommodation in the heart of Connemara.
✉ Off the N59 5km from Recess ☎ 095-31006; www.ballynahinch-castle.com
🕐 Closed 15–27 Dec; 29 Jan–23 Feb

Bunratty
Co Clare

Bunratty Woods Country House (€–€€)
Situated in the grounds of the historic Bunratty Castle, this guesthouse contains many interesting antiques and has mountain views.
✉ Low Road ☎ 061-369689
🕐 Closed 7 Nov–early Mar

Cashel
Co Galway

Cashel House (€€–€€€)
Gracious country house hotel in award-winning gardens overlooking Cashel Bay.
✉ Off the N59, 1.5km west of Recess ☎ 095-31001; www.cashel-house-hotel.com
🕐 Closed early Jan–early Feb

Clifden
Co Galway

Rock Glen (€€)
Traditional hospitality and excellent cuisine are provided in this beautifully converted shooting lodge.
☎ 095-21035; www.rockglenhotel.com
🕐 Closed 6 weeks between Jan and Mar

Doolin
Co Clare

Aran View House (€–€€)
This comfortable hotel is set in farmland, with views of the Aran Islands.
✉ Coast Road ☎ 065-7074061; www.aranview.com
🕐 Closed end Oct–Easter

Ennistymon
Co Clare

Grovemount House (€)
A purpose-built guesthouse on the edge of the town, convenient for both The Burren and the Clare coast.
✉ Lahinch Road ☎ 065-7071431 🕐 Closed Nov–May

Galway
Co Galway

Eyre Square Hotel (€€–€€€)
This hotel is in a central location and offers fine accommodation.
✉ Forster Street, off Eyre Square ☎ 091 569633; www.byrne-hotels_ireland.com
🕐 Closed 25–6 Dec

Glenlo Abbey (€€€)
Occupying an 18th-century abbey and in a landscaped estate overlooking a lough.
✉ Bushypark ☎ 091-526666; www.glenlo.com

White House (€)
A purpose-built guesthouse overlooking Galway Bay and The Burren, it has large, well equipped bedrooms.
✉ 2 Ocean Wave, Salthill ☎ 091 529399; www.oceanbb.com

Roundstone
Co Galway

Eldon's (€–€€)
A distinctive blue-and-yellow painted building in this picturesque fishing village, Eldon's has a restaurant that specialises in local seafood.
✉ Main Street ☎ 095-35933; www.eldons.ie
🕐 Closed Jan

The North

Armagh
Co Armagh
Hillview Lodge (££)

Family-run guesthouse with good facilities in a rural setting just a mile from the city. Golf driving range.

✉ 33 Newtownhamilton Road
☎ 028 3752 2000;
www.hillviewlodge.com

Ballintoy
Co Antrim
Whitepark House (££)

Country house on the coast road between the Causeway and the rope bridge.

✉ 150 Whitepark Road
☎ 028 2073 1482;
www.whiteparkhouse.com

Belfast
Ash-Rowan Town House (££)

Former home of Thomas Andrews, designer of the *Titanic*. The quality furnishings certainly go down well with guests here.

✉ 12 Windsor Avenue
☎ 028 9066 1758

Jury's Belfast Inn (££)

In the heart of the city adjacent to the Opera House, a short walk from the main shopping area.

✉ Fisherwick Place, Great Victoria Street ☎ 028 9053 3500; www.jurysdoyle.com

Malmaison Belfast (£££)

This luxury hotel has an Italianate façade and superb styled bedrooms.

✉ 34–38 Victoria Street
☎ 028 9022 0200;
www.malmaison.com

Carnlough
Co Antrim
Londonderry Arms Hotel (££–£££)

Famous for its food and its history, this fine Georgian house was once owned by Sir Winston Churchill.

✉ 20 Harbour Road
☎ 028 2888 5255;
www.glensofantrim.com

Coleraine
Co Londonderry
Breezemount House (££)

Restored 19th-century house offering superior bed-and-breakfast facilities. All rooms have en-suite bathroom, own kitchen and satellite TV.

✉ 26 Castlerock Road
☎ 028 7034 4615;
www.breezemount.co.uk
🕐 Closed 24–8 Dec

Donegal
Co Donegal
Central Hotel (€€–€€€)

Family-run town-centre hotel with views over Donegal Bay from the garden.

✉ The Diamond
☎ 074-9721027;
www.whites-hotelsireland.com

Harvey's Point (€€)

On Lough Eske's shore, this modern hotel has spacious bedrooms and fine cuisine.

✉ Lough Eske, on N56
☎ 074-9722208;
www.harveyspoint.com
🕐 Closed Mon–Tue Nov–Mar

Enniskillen
Co Fermanagh
Arch House Tullyhona (£)

Comfortable, award-winning guesthouse, good for families with young children.

✉ 59 Marble Arch Road
☎ 028 6634 8452;
www.archhouse.com

Londonderry
Co Londonderry
Trinity Hotel (£££)

Bright new city-centre hotel.

✉ 22–24 Strand Road
☎ 028 7127 1271

Hastings Europa Hotel (£££)

Most hotels strive for recognition and are only too pleased to be described with superlatives, but Belfast's Europa Hotel cannot have been too delighted with its one-time fame – as 'the most bombed hotel'. On the bright side, this has resulted in splendid refurbishment, so that the Europa is now a truly international hotel with excellent facilities and was the choice of President Clinton during his visit to Belfast.

✉ Great Victoria Street
☎ 028 9027 1066;
www.hastingshotels.com

Shopping Centres & Department Stores

Tax-Free Shopping
Non-EU visitors to Ireland (both the Republic and Northern Ireland) can shop tax-free in certain stores. Where you see the Tax-Free sticker, ask for a cashback voucher every time you make a purchase. You then present these vouchers at the cashback desk at Dublin or Shannon airports for an immediate refund. If you are leaving from another airport or by ferry, you need to ask the store for a pre-paid cashback envelope so that you can send your vouchers for a cheque or credit card refund.

On the whole, shopping malls are the same in every town, but if you want to find everything under one roof, Ireland has some good examples to choose from.

Dublin
There are large malls at Blackrock (a short walk from DART Blackrock station), Blanchardstown (north on the N3), the Liffey Valley Centre (west off the N4 just beyond the M50 interchange) and The Square at Tallaght (south off the N81), which has over 130 outlets and a multi-screen cinema. These are the city-centre malls:

ILAC Centre
At the heart of the northside redevelopment scheme, this centre has a good range of outlets, including Dunnes and Roches.
✉ **Off Henry Street** ☎ **01-7041460** 🕐 **Daily 9–6:30 (to 9PM Thu, Fri)**

Jervis Centre
On the northside. Renowned for having lots of UK chains.
✉ **125 Upper Abbey Street**
☎ **01-8781323**

Powerscourt Townhouse
A departure from the usual shopping mall, this elegant conversion of a historic townhouse has quality shops and eateries around a courtyard. Live piano music daily and special events.
✉ **South William Street**
☎ **01-6794144** 🕐 **Mon–Sat 9–6 (to 7PM Thu)**

St Stephen's Green Shopping Centre
Huge, modern centre with over 100 shops on three floors, a large car park, restaurants, pubs and cafés.
✉ **St Stephen's Green, at junction with Grafton Street and South King Street** ☎ **01-4780888** 🕐 **Mon–Sat 9–7 (to 9PM Thu, 8PM Fri), Sun 12–7**

East

Waterford
City Square Shopping Centre
A good variety of department stores, high-street chains, fashion and specialist shops.
☎ **051-853528**

South

Cork
Merchant's Quay Shopping Centre
✉ **1 Patrick Street**

Killarney Outlet Centre
✉ **Fair Hill, Killarney**

West

Bunratty, Co Clare
Bunratty Village Mills
Opened in 1998, with a variety of shops, many selling Irish craft work.
☎ **061-364321** 🕐 **Daily**

Galway, Co Galway
Eyre Square Shopping Centre
A bright development which incorporates part of the old city walls, where an antiques market is held every Sunday.
☎ **091-568302** 🕐 **Mon–Sat 9–6:30 (to 9PM Thu and Fri). Sun 12–6**

Galway Shopping Centre
Over 60 shops under cover and just 10 minutes' walk from Eyre Square. Also has a popular 10-pin bowling alley.
✉ **Headford Road**

Limerick
Arthur's Quay Shopping Centre
Very attractive collection of over 30 stores in a prime city-centre location; restaurants, crèche and play area and plenty of parking.

North

Belfast
Castle Court
Northern Ireland's largest complex is in the heart of Belfast. It's sparklingly modern and has all kinds of shops on two levels.
✉ **Royal Avenue** ☎ **028 9023 4591** 🕐 **Mon–Sat 9–6 (to 9PM Thu), Sun 1–6**

Forestside Shopping Centre
All the usual high-street stores, including Sainsbury's supermarket, open 24 hours. Over 1,000 parking spaces
✉ **Upper Galwally** ✉ **028 9049 4990** 🕐 **Mon–Wed 9–9, Thu–Fri 9AM–10PM, Sat 9–7, Sun 1–6**

Westwood Shopping Centre
In west Belfast near the M1 junction, a bright centre with all the usual chains.
✉ **Kennedy Way** ☎ **028 9061 1255** 🕐 **Mon–Sat 8–6 (supermarkets open until 10PM, Fri 11PM), Sun 1–6**

Londonderry
Lisnagelvin Shopping Centre
Good selection of large and small stores. Easy access.
✉ **Waterside** 🕐 **Mon–Tue 9–8, Wed–Fri 9–9, Sat 9–5:30**

Northside Shopping Centre
A winning blend of old and new gives this centre a comfortable atmosphere for shopping.
✉ **Glangalliagh Road** 🕐 **Mon–Sat 9–5:30 (to 9PM Thu and Fri)**

Department Stores
East

Dublin
Arnotts
A major refurbishment has put this store at the forefront of the new-look northside.
✉ **12 Henry Street** ☎ **01-8050400** 🕐 **Mon–Sat 6–6.30 (to 9.30 Thu), Sun 12–6**

Brown Thomas
Sophisticated store, with top quality goods, including designer fashions and cosmetics. Cafés and a hair salon.
✉ **88–92 Grafton Street** ☎ **01-6056666** 🕐 **Mon–Sat 9–8 (to 9PM on Thu), Sun 10–7**

Clery's
Ireland's only remaining Irish-owned department store; as well as all the usual things, it is good for souvenirs.
✉ **O'Connell Street** ☎ **01-8786000** 🕐 **Mon–Sat 9–6:30 (to 9PM Thu, 8PM Fri) Sun 12–6**

West

Galway
Anthony Ryan's
All the usual departments, but specialises in women's wear.
✉ **6–18 Shop Street** ☎ **091-567061**

Penneys
Fashions for everyone, good accessories department and household wares.
✉ **Eyre Square Centre** ☎ **091-566889/565095**

North

Donegal
Magee's
Run by the same family since 1866. The speciality is hand-woven Donegal tweed; guided tours of original looms at work.
✉ **The Diamond, Donegal Town** ☎ **074-9722660**

Modern Shopping
The Square Towncentre at Tallaght, just south of Dublin, is a superb modern shopping centre, the largest in Ireland, with nearly 150 shops under a huge dome of natural light. Trees and shrubs thrive in these conditions, creating an illusion of the outdoors where it never rains. The centre, open every day, also includes a 12-screen cinema, restaurants, a free crèche and free parking for 3,000 cars.

Crafts

Quality Crafts
The Irish pride in fine craftsmanship is reflected in the number of visitor attractions that offer quality crafts in their gift shops. Right alongside the souvenir key rings and packets of shamrock seed you will find glittering crystal, fine pottery, linen, Celtic jewellery and beautiful tweeds and woollens. The same is true of the major tourist information centres, which offer a splendid showcase for Irish goods.

Linen Goods
Irish linen is known all over the world, but the industry suffered enormously with the advent of new, cheaper fibres. Though it is unlikely that it will ever achieve the heights of its 19th-century heyday, the linen industry is enjoying a renewed interest, and fine quality goods are still being produced in Northern Ireland.

East

Dublin

Cleo
Clothes made in knitters' and weavers' homes from natural fibres of Irish origin.
✉ 18 Kildare Street ☎ 01-6761421 🕐 Mon–Sat 9–5:30

Design Yard
Features some of the best contemporary Irish craft workers and innovative artists styling in glass, metal, ceramic and wood.
✉ Cow's Lane, Temple Bar ☎ 01-4741011 🕐 Daily 10–5:30

Kilkenny Centre
Made in Ireland is the key. Large selection of pottery, jewellery, glassware and fashion items. Traditional but with a touch of new creativity.
✉ 6–10 Nassau Street ☎ 01-6777066 🕐 Mon–Sat 8:30–7, Sun 11–6

Avoca, Co Wicklow
Avoca Handweavers
The oldest working woollen mill in Ireland. All kinds of Irish-made crafts. Tea room.
✉ Avoca ☎ 01-2867466 🕐 Daily 9:30–5:30

Kilkenny, Co Kilkenny
Kilkenny Design Centre
Superb range of top quality crafts from all over Ireland.
✉ Castle Yard, Kilkenny ☎ 056-7722118 ✉ Mon–Sat 10–7, Sun 11–7. Closed Jan–early Apr

Kilmore Quay, Co Wexford
Country Crafts
A good selection of pottery, paintings and local crafts.
✉ Kilmore Quay ☎ 053-29885

🕐 Daily 10–7 high season, (11–5 mid-season), Sat and Sun 11–5 low season

Newtowncashel, Co Longford
Carving Bogwood Sculpture
Beautiful sculptures; video and photographs tell story of the 5,000-year-old bogwood.
✉ Barley Harbour ☎ 043-25297 🕐 Mon–Sat 9–6

South

Adare, Co Limerick
Black Abbey Crafts
Good selection of quality Irish cafts – ceramics, slate, iron and glass items.
✉ Adare ☎ 061-396021 🕐 Mon–Sun 10–6

Blarney, Co Cork
Blarney Woollen Mills
First established in 1750, the company now offers woven rugs and Aran sweaters, plus crystal,china and gifts.
✉ Blarney ☎ 021-4516111

Carrick-on-Suir, Co Tipperary
Tipperary Crystal Craft
Two thatched cottages house workshops where crystal is made. Watch glass-blowing and -moulding.
✉ Ballynoran ☎ 051-641188 🕐 Daily 9:30–6

West

Carron, Co Clare
Burren Perfumery
Demonstrations of essential oil extraction. Audio visual, photographic exhibition, shop, organic herb garden and tea rooms.
✉ Carron ☎ 065-7089102 🕐 Daily 9–5 (Jun–Sep to 7); sometimes closed Jan

Dingle
Louis Mulcahy Pottery
This renowned pottery sells quality lampshades, sculpted masks and more.

✉ **Clogher Head** ☎ **066-9156229;**
www.louismulcahy.com
🕐 Daily, May–Jun 9–7; Jul–Aug 9–8; 9–6 rest of year

Doolin, Co Clare
Doolin Crafts Gallery
Crafts gallery run by batik artist and jewellery designer. Also sells weaving and Irish instruments. Restaurant.

✉ **Doolin** ☎ **065-7074309**
🕐 Daily (restaurant Apr–Oct)

Foxford, Co Mayo
Foxford Woollen Mills Visitor Centre
Take a tour of the historic woollen mill. Also houses jewellery and woodcraft workshops and art gallery.

✉ **Foxford** ☎ **094-9256104**

Galway, Co Galway
Tús Craft Design Shop
This craft co-op centre displays ceramics, stained glass, painted silks, jewellery and delightful fairy dolls.

✉ **Bridge Mills, Bridge Street**
☎ **091-532500** 🕐 Mon–Sat 10–6

Roundstone
IDA Centre
Music, fashion and craft shops including pottery and jewellery. *Bodhrán* making demonstrations. Café.

✉ **Roundstone** ☎ **095-35875**

Shannon, Co Clare
Ballycasey Craft & Design Centre
Craftspeople here include: potters, goldsmith, dress designer, florist and framer.

✉ **Shannon** ☎ **061-364115**

North

Adara, Co Donegal
Bonners of Adara
Bonners, world-renowned for the quality of their knitwear, have a factory in the town and employ hand-knitters throughout Donegal. Also sells Waterford Crystal, Belleek and Donegal china, jewellery, linens and tweeds.

✉ **Front Street** ☎ **074-9541303** 🕐 May–Jun Mon–Sat 9–6:30; Jul–Aug Mon–Sat 10–7, Sun 10–6; Sep–Apr Mon–Tue Thu–Sat 10–6

Belfast
Conway Mill Craft Shop
Over 22 artists work within this old mill. Items of contemporary and Irish art. Also guided tours of the mill.

✉ **5–7 Conway Street** ☎ **028 9032 6452** 🕐 Mon–Fri 10–4

The Wicker Man
Highly regarded craft shop showcasing work by over 150 Irish craftspeople.

✉ **14 Donegal Arcade, Castle Place** ☎ **028 9024 3550**
🕐 Mon–Sat 9–5:30 (to 9PM Thu)

Donegal, Co Donegal
Donegal Craft Village
Variety of items, including pottery, Uilleann pipes, jewellery, batik and woven goods. Coffee shop.

✉ **Ballyshannon Road** ☎ **074-9722225** 🕐 Mon–Sat 10–5:30 (sometimes closed winter)

Dungannon, Co Tyrone
Tyrone Crystal
Guided tour takes in all the stages of producing fine crystal, from glass-blowing to cutting and finishing.

✉ **Killybrackey, Coalisland Rd**
☎ **028 8772 5335** 🕐 Shop: Mon–Sat 9:30–5, Sun 1–5 (seasonal). Tours: Mon–Fri 11, 12, 2 & 3

Londonderry, Co Londonderry
Derry Craft Village
Craftspeople ply their trades in an 18th-century setting.

✉ **Shipquay Street** ☎ **028-7126 0329** 🕐 Daily 9–6/7

Kilkenny Workshops
Frequently while driving through rural Ireland, you will see signs for craft workshops, but Co Kilkenny is particularly well endowed with them. The Kilkenny Design Workshops began the resurgence of high quality Irish crafts in the 1960s, and their example attracted many talented artists and craft workers to the area.

Linen Mill Visits
The best way to visit the working linen mills is on the Irish Linen tour, a six-hour trip which includes lunch and a knowledgeable guide. Tours leave Banbridge Gateway Tourist Information Centre on Wednesday and Saturday between May and September.

Traditional Music, Antiques & Markets

Dublin Bargain-hunting
There are lots of antiques shops and stalls in Dublin. The famous locations are Francis Street and Powerscourt Townhouse, but you are unlikely to find any bargains there. Instead look alongside the Liffey, particularly Ormond Quay and Bachelors Walk.

Traditional Music

East

Dublin
Celtic Note
Small, specialist Irish music store featuring everything from folk and traditional ballads to rock and contemporary.
✉ **12 Nassau Street**
☎ **01-6704157**

Claddagh Records
CDs and tapes including Irish dance bands.
✉ **Cecelia Street, Temple Bar**
☎ **01677-0262**

South

Cork, Co Cork
Living Tradition
The music shop of Ossian Music Company. Traditional instruments, sheet music, CDs, cassettes and videos.
✉ **40 MacCurtain Street**
☎ **021-4502040**

Kenmare, Co Kerry
The Sounds of Music
Good range of CDs including traditional Irish music and a selection of instruments.
✉ **Henry Street** ☎ **064-42268**

Killarney, Co Kerry
Variety Sounds
A wide range of traditional Irish instruments, CDs and tutor books.
✉ **7 College Street**
☎ **064-35755**

West

Ennis, Co Clare
Custy's Traditional Music Shop
Owned and staffed by experts.
✉ **Francis St** ☎ **065-6821727**

Galway, Co Galway
Mulligans
Stocks just about every traditional Irish music recording ever made, also jazz, blues, soul and country music.
✉ **5 Middle Street**
☎ **091-564961**

North

Belfast
Premier Record Store
Specialises in traditional CDs and tapes. Behind Castle Court Shopping Centre.
✉ **3–5 Smithfield Square North**
☎ **028 9024 0896**

Londonderry, Co Londonderry
Stillsounds
Every genre of music is catered for here, both new and second hand.
✉ **22A Waterloo Street**
☎ **028 7128 8890**

Antiques

East

Dublin
Timepiece Antique Clocks
Mostly 18th- & 19th-century Irish clocks, restored and sold on the premises.
✉ **57–58 Patrick Street**
☎ **01-4540774**

John Farrington Antiques
This small shop is packed with Irish furniture, silver, glass and *objets d'art*. The precious antique jewellery is especially coveted.
✉ **32 Drury Street**
☎ **01-6791899**

Silver Shop
Wide range of antique silver and silver-plate from the

WHERE TO SHOP

conventional to the unusual.
Great for imaginative gifts.

✉ **1st Floor, Powerscourt Townhouse Centre, Clarendon Street** ☎ 01-6794147

South

Tralee, Co Kerry
O'Keef's Antiques
Antiquarian books, paintings, silver and more.

✉ **15 Princes Quay**
☎ 066-7125635

Adare, Co Limerick
George Stackpole
Antiques and books, bought and sold.

✉ **Main Street**
☎ 061-396409

West

Galway, Co Galway
Tempo Antiques
Small antiques, jewellery, procelain and collectable gifts.

✉ **9 Cross Street**
☎ 091-562282

Tolco Antiques
Antiques from Georgian to Edwardian eras.

✉ **Headford Road**
☎ 091-751146

North

Belfast
Oakland Antiques
On two floors, this is the place to find period furniture, silver, clocks, porcelain, glass and quality paintings.

✉ **135 Donegall Pass**
☎ 028 9023 0176

Markets

Most country towns will have a traditional market, usually offering a mixture of good local produce, cheap imported clothing and sometimes livestock. A good place to experience the everyday life of the local community. Enquire locally for specific days.

East

Blackrock, Co Dublin
Blackrock Market
Lively traditional market every weekend.

✉ **Main Street** ☎ 01-2833522

Dublin
Meeting House Square Food Market
Wonderful array of Irish and international food. Every Saturday except Christmas.

✉ **Meeting House Square, Temple Bar**

Mother Redcap's Market
Books, antiques, clothes, music, cakes and cheeses.

✉ **Back Lane (opposite Christ Church Cathedral)**

Temple Bar Book Market
Large selection of old and new titles on Saturdays.

✉ **Meeting House Square**

South

Cork, Co Cork
The English Market
Covered market with array of food stalls daily.

✉ **Princes Street/Patrick Street/Grand Parade**

Limerick, Co Limerick
Milk Market
Retail outlets open all week; arts and crafts market on Friday; traditional market Saturday morning.

✉ **Corn Market Row**

West

Galway, Co Galway
Antique Market
Antiques and bric-à-brac.

✉ **Eyre Square Centre**

North

Belfast
St George's Market
Built in 1896, the market has had a facelift. Open Friday morning and Saturday 10–4.

✉ **Oxford Street/May Street**

Undercover Market
The English Market, off Patrick Street, is one of Cork's old institutions and is great fun to stroll through. It is a huge undercover market packed with stalls, mostly selling foodstuffs of a traditional Irish nature, though a few more exotic items have begun to appear.

109

Children's Attractions

Exciting Sightseeing
If your children groan when they hear the word 'sightseeing', you can surprise them with an exciting tour of Dublin in an ex-World War II amphibious vehicle. It starts at St Patrick's Cathedral or St Stephen's Green North and takes in all the main city-centre sights – then heads straight into the waters of Grand Canal Basin to finish the tour afloat.

Viking Splash Tour
✉ 64–65 Patrick Street
☎ 01-7076000;
www.vikingsplashtours.com
🕐 Every half hour 10–12,
1:30–5. Mar–Oct daily; Feb
Wed–Sun; Nov Tue–Sun

East

Dublin

Bram Stoker Dracula Experience

All the latest technology gives you a spine-chilling encounter with Count Dracula in rooms such as 'Time Tunnel to Transylvania' and the 'Blood Laboratory'.
✉ Westwood Club, Clontarf
Road ☎ 01-8057824
🕐 Fri–Sun noon–10

Dublin Zoo

This historic zoo in Phoenix Park makes an ideal family day out.
✉ Phoenix Park ☎ 01-474
8900 🕐 Mar–Sep: Mon–Sat
9:30–6, Sun 10:30–6. Oct–Feb:
Mon–Sat 9:30–dusk, Sun 10:30–
dusk 🍽 Restaurant, cafés,
kiosks (€) 🚌 No 10 bus from
O'Connell Street 🚻 Good
🎟 Expensive

South

Ballyporeen, Co Tipperary

Mitchelstown Caves

The caves are renowned for their depth of 1km, and comprise two groups, Desmond's Cave and New Cave. Electric lighting casts mysterious shadows.
✉ Off the N8 4km north of
Ballyporeen ☎ 052-67246
🕐 Mar–Nov 10–6; Dec–Feb
11–4:30 🚌 Buses from Dublin
to Cork pass through
Mitchelstown 🎟 Moderate

Clonakilty, Co Cork

Clonakilty Model Village

A miniature working railway that depicts the Old West Cork Railway and travels around the model village. Also life-size train rides around the village or to the town and Inchydoney.
✉ The Station, Inchydoney
Road ☎ 023-33224 🕐
Feb–Oct daily 11–5 (Jul–Aug
10–6) 🚻 Good 🎟 Village
moderate; train rides expensive

Dingle, Co Kerry

Dingle Oceanworld

Underwater life galore. Watch out for the sharks!
✉ Dingle Harbour
☎ 066-9152111 🕐 Jul–Aug
9–8:30; May, Jun, Sep 9–6:30;
Oct–Apr 10–5 🚌 From Tralee
🚻 Good 🎟 Expensive

Fota, Co Cork

Fota Wildlife Park

Established by the Royal Zoological Society of Ireland, Fota Wildlife Park's primary aim is the breeding of endangered species. It is an open park – except for the cheetah!
✉ 1.5km south of Cork Harbour
☎ 021-4812678 🕐 Daily 10–5
🚻 Few 🎟 Expensive

Limerick, Co Limerick

Peter Pan Funworld

This is an indoor paradise for young children, with a huge ball pool, giant bouncy castle and lots of things to clamber on and slide down.
✉ Crescent Shopping Centre,
Dooradoyle ☎ 061-301033
🕐 Daily 10–7
🎟 Expensive

Tralee, Co Kerry

Aqua Dome

Tralee's wonderful waterpark has all the rides you would expect. You can also visit the Blennerville Windmill.
✉ On the Dingle road
☎ Aqua Dome: 066-7128899
🕐 Aqua Dome Mon–Fri 10–10,
Sat, Sun 11–8; windmill Apr–Oct
10–6 🎟 Expensive

West

Castlebar, Co Mayo
Mayo Leisure Point
The largest indoor leisure complex in Ireland including bowling, adventure slides and 7-screen cinema.
✉ Moneen ☎ 094-9025473
🕐 Daily (telephone for details)
♿ Good 💷 Varies

Lahinch, Co Clare
Seaworld
Leisure centre, aquarium and swimming pool.
✉ The Promenade ☎ 065-7081900 🕐 Daily (telephone for details) 🍴 Refreshments (€) ♿ Good 💷 Moderate

Salthill, Co Galway
Leisureland
A modern pool complex with waterslides and playground.
☎ 091-521455 🕐 Mon–Fri 8–10, Sat 8–5, Sun 8–6
💷 Moderate

Shannonbridge
Clonmacnoise & West Offaly Railway
Narrow-gauge railway tour of the Blackwater bog (9km) with on-board commentary.
☎ 090-9674114 🕐 Apr–Oct daily 10–5, trains leave on the hour. Groups only in winter
🍴 Coffee shop (€) ♿ Few
💷 Moderate

North

Ballymoney, Co Antrim
Leslie Hill Open Farm
Horse and trap rides, rare breeds, nature trails, lake, museum, playgrounds.
✉ Macfin Road ☎ 028 2766 6803 🕐 Easter weekend & May Sun & public hols 2–6; Jun Sat–Sun 2–6; Jul–Aug Mon–Sat 11–6, Sun 2–6 🍴 Tea room (£)
♿ Few 💷 Moderate

Belfast
Aunt Sandra's Candy Factory
Through a viewing window at the candy factory, you can watch traditional sweets being made by hand – then buy some to take home.
✉ 60 Castlereagh Road
☎ 028 9073 2868 🕐 Mon–Fri 9:30–4:30, Sat 9:30–5
🚌 Citybus 32 💷 Free

Belfast Zoo
A modern world-class zoo set in attractive parkland and housing over 160 species of rare and endangered animals.
✉ Off Antrim Road ☎ 028 9077 6277 🕐 Apr–Sep daily 10–5; Oct–Mar daily 10–2:30 🍴 Refreshments (£) 🚌 Metro 1a, 1b, 1c, 1d, 1f, 2a from city centre
♿ Good 💷 Moderate

W5
An interactive discovery centre located at the Odyssey in central Belfast. Five exhibition areas 'Wow, Start, Go, See and Do'.
✉ 2 Queen's Quay ☎ 028 9046 7700 🕐 Mon–Sat 10–6, Sun 12–6 🚌 City airport bus
♿ Good 💷 Moderate

Portaferry, Co Down
Exploris
One of Europe's finest aquariums with a huge Open Sea Tank with side views, touch tanks, and other attractions.
✉ The Rope Walk ☎ 028 4272 8062 🕐 Mon–Fri 10–6, Sat 11–6, Sun 1–6 (5 in winter)
🍴 Tea room (£) ♿ Good
💷 Moderate

Portrush, Co Down
Dunluce Centre
Refurbished in 2002, the centre features Finn McCool Playground, a themed and interactive game environment for all abilities. Also, Treasure Fortress and Turbo Tours for thrills.
✉ 10 Sandhill Drive ☎ 028 7082 4444 🕐 Apr–May Sat–Sun 12–6:30; Jun Mon–Fri 10–5, Sat–Sun 12–6:30; Jul–Aug daily 10:30–6:30; Sep–Mar Sat–Sun 12–5 💷 Moderate

Story-telling
'Tell me a story' is a request that would hardly ever go unheeded in Ireland – often you don't even need to ask – and story-telling is a tradition that goes back far beyond the written word. Ancient myths and legends have been perpetuated in many forms and new stories added. The art of story-telling is still alive in parts of the west and south, and all ages are enthralled. Three interesting story-telling festivals are the Sean McCarthy Memorial Week in Listowel, Co Kerry, in August, one on Cape Clear, Co Cork, in September, and at the Mid-Ulster Folk Festival at Springhill House, Moneymore, County Londonderry, in October.

Live Music & Nightclubs

Music Sessions

Traditional music sessions are widespread throughout Ireland, but the west has a particularly rich heritage. Some city pubs will have a session every night, with different musicians at each, and even in the country there will be a session somewhere within easy reach. Sessions are informal and unrehearsed, but the fiddlers, flautists, whistlers, pipers, *bodhrán* players and whoever else may turn up all know the tunes and standards are usually very high.

Live Music

There is live music all over Ireland every night of the week. Here are just a few recommendations:

East

Dublin

O'Shea's Merchant
Traditional music and dancing. You'll be encouraged to dance.
✉ **12 Lower Bridge Street**
☎ **01-6796793**

The Point
Vast venue in former tram depot attracts music and dance superstars.
✉ **East Link Bridge, North Wall Quay** ☎ **01-8366777**

Temple Bar Music Centre
A music venue that also hosts club nights, live music, dances and fashion shows.
✉ **Curved Street**
☎ **01-6709202**

Whelans
Famous Dublin music venue, hosting traditional Irish, rock, jazz and blues.
✉ **25 Wexford Street**
☎ **01-4780766**

Glencullen Co Dublin

Johnnie Foxes
Music every day.
☎ **01-2955647**

South

Clonakilty, Co Cork

De Barra's Pub
Famous landmark pub featuring the best in live folk and traditional music.
✉ **Pearse Street**
☎ **023-33381**

Cork, Co Cork

Lobby Bar
Traditional music of Ireland and elsewhere. Concert venue upstairs.
✉ **1 Union Quay**
☎ **021-4311113**

The Old Oak Bar
Award-winning music venue. Live bands and traditional sessions on two floors.
✉ **113 Oliver Plunkett Street**
☎ **0121-4276165**

Dingle, Co Kerry

Dingle An Droichead Beag
Dingle's musical mecca.
✉ **Main Street** ☎ **066-9151723**

Kenmare, Co Kerry

Crowley's
If it's tradition you are seeking you'll find it here in the heart of Kenmare. Impromptu Irish music sessions take place regularly.
✉ **Henry Street** ☎ **064-41472**

Limerick Co Limerick

The Warehouse
Live music venue, located behind a pub which has traditional music and dancing.
✉ **Behind Dolan's Pub, Alphonsus Street, off Dock Road**
☎ **061-314483**

West

Galway, Co Galway

Bar Cuba
Latin American and jazz.
✉ **Eyre Square**
☎ **091-565991**

The Roisin Dubh
Traditional Irish, rock and pop in pub and on stage.
✉ **8 Upper Dominick Street**
☎ **091-586540** ◉ **Nightly**

Tigh Colí
Traditional music venue.
✉ **Mainguard Street** ☎ **091-561294** 🕐 **Nightly 6 and 9:30**

North

Belfast
John Hewitt Bar
In the heart of the Cathedral quarter, this very traditional bar stages jazz on Friday and traditional music on Tuesday, Wednesday and Saturday.
✉ **51 Donegall Street**
☎ **028 9023 3768**

Robinsons
Northern Ireland Music Pub of the Year in 1998. Five bars, each with a style.
✉ **38–42 Great Victoria Street**
☎ **028 9024 7447**

Rotterdam Bar
Probably the most famous of Belfast's music pubs. Bands play outside in summer, attracting huge crowds into Barrow Square.
✉ **54 Pilot Street** ☎ **028 9074 6021**

Londonderry
Co Londonderry
Dungloe Bar
✉ **Waterloo Street**
☎ **028 7126 7716**

Nightclubs

East

Dublin
Club M
Lively venue in the centre of Temple Bar. Mainstream chart hits for late night groovers. The lighting system is worth it alone.
✉ **Blooms Hotel, 6 Anglesea Street** ☎ **01-6715622**

Lillie's Bordello
One of Dublin's most popular and well-established clubs featuring house, chart and oldie music.
✉ **Adam Court, Grafton Street**
☎ **01-6799204**

POD
The Place of Dance remains one of the hippest clubs in town. There is a different club each evening.
✉ **35 Harcourt Street**
☎ **01-4780225**

South

Cork, Co Cork
Newport
Late-night funky lounge and adjacent nightclub.
✉ **Paul Street Plaza** ☎ **021-4254872/4**

West

Galway, Co Galway
Boo Radley's Nightclub
Clubbers can dance to music of top DJ's on three floors.
✉ **Eyre Square Hotel, Forster Street** ☎ **091-569633**

GPO
Music varies depending on which night you go: 70s disco, country, dance acts.
✉ **Eglington Street**
☎ **091-563073; www.gpo.ie**

Salthill, Co Galway
Warwick
Live bands and DJs draw in the crowds.
✉ **O'Connor's, Warwick Hotel**
☎ **091-521244** 🕐 **Fri, Sat from 11PM**

North

Belfast
The Fly Bar
Sophisticated cocktails and Cool FM DJs.
✉ **5–6 Lower Crescent**
☎ **028 9050 9750**

Front Page
Pub club with live bands.
✉ **Lower Donegall Street**
☎ **028 9032 4924**

Club Milk
Offers a varied spectrum of music from house to disco.
✉ **10–14 Tomb Street** ☎ **028 9027 8876** 🕐 **Nightly**

Buskers
Dublin's Grafton Street is famous as much for its buskers as for its excellent shopping. The variety of open-air acts is enormous, and in strolling the length of the street you might hear such diverse sounds as a lone penny whistle playing traditional jigs and reels, a classical string quartet, a South American band or a jazz or rock guitarist. The quality varies too, but all are hugely entertaining and contribute to the street's unique atmosphere.

Theatres & Cinemas

Festivals

The number and variety of Irish festivals – both internationally important and small local events – is enormous. Music festivals include classical, opera, jazz, country and western and traditional Irish music and dancing, sometimes with competitions for pipers and *bodhrán* players. Arts festivals encompass drama, poetry readings and literary competitions. There are sporting festivals, including horse-racing, golf, sailing and angling; there are also gourmet festivals, film festivals and flower festivals. Many take place in the summer, but visitors will find something going on somewhere in every month of the year.

Theatres

East

Dublin
Gaiety
Pantomime, opera, musicals, plays, comedies.
✉ **South King Street**
☎ **01-6771717**

South

Cork, Co Cork
Triskal Arts Centre
Drama, readings, children's theatre and music.
✉ **Tobin Street**
☎ **021-4272022**

Bantry, Co Cork
Cinemax
✉ **The Quay** ☎ **027-55777;**
www.cinemaxbantry.com

Tralee, Co Kerry
Siamsa Tire – The National Folk Theatre of Ireland
Keeping the national traditions alive.
✉ **Town Park** ☎ **066-7123055**

Waterford, Co Waterford
Theatre Royal
Hosts the Opera Festival and The Waterford Show.
✉ **The Mall** ☎ **051-874402**

West

Galway, Co Galway
Claddagh Hall
Traditional music and dance and folk drama.
✉ **Nimmos Pier** ☎ **091-755479/588044/755888** 🕐 **Mid-Jun to early Sep 8:45PM**

North

Belfast
Old Museum Arts Centre
Experimental theatre, dance, story-telling, and poetry.
✉ **College Square North**
☎ **028 9023 3332**

Londonderry,
Verbal Arts Centre
Children's events, storytelling and more.
✉ **London Street**
☎ **028 7126 6946**

Cinemas

East

Dublin
Irish Film Institute
✉ **6 Eustace Street, Temple Bar** ☎ **01-6795744; www.fii.ie**

South

Limerick, Co Limerick
Savoy Limerick Cineplex
✉ **Bedford Row** ☎ **061-311900 (recorded information)**

West

Galway, Co Calway
Galway Omniplex
Premiere cinema complex with the latest technology in projection and sound.
✉ **Headford Road**
☎ **091-567800**

North

Belfast
The Movie House
✉ **Yorkgate Shopping Complex, York Street**
☎ **028 9075 5000**

Queen's Film Theatre
✉ **University Square Mews**
☎ **028-9097 1097**

Londonderry
Nerve Centre
Innovative arts centre.
☎ **028 7126 0562**

Sports

Ireland's contribution to the sporting world has always been disproportionate to her size. In sports as varied as fottball, snooker, golf and horse racing, the Irish are world leaders.

Irish Sports Council
✉ 21 Fitzwilliam Square, Dublin 2 ☎ 01-8608800

Sports Council of Northern Ireland
✉ House of Sport, Upper Malone Road, Belfast
☎ 028 9038 1222

Gaelic Sports

Cumann Luthchleas Gael
✉ Pairc an Chrocaigh, Dublin 3 ☎ 01-8363222

Gaelic Athletic Association
✉ Belfast ☎ 028 3752 1907

Golf

There are over 400 golf courses in Ireland. Standards and regulations vary, so it is best to get advance information:

Golfing Union of Ireland
The Republic of Ireland's golfing body can give details on all Ireland's courses.
✉ Unit 8, Block G, Maynooth Business Campus, Maynooth Co Kildare ☎ 01505 4000; www.gui.ie

Greyhound-racing

This is a popular spectator sport throughout Ireland.

Irish Greyhound Board
☎ www.igb.ie

Horse-racing

Horse-racing is very popular in the Republic of Ireland, and full details race courses

are available from:
Horse Racing Authority
✉ Leopardstown Racecourse, Foxrock, Dublin 18
☎ 01-2893607

Down Royal Racecourse
Ireland's premier racecourse. Meetings include the Ulster Oaks and the Ulster Derby.
✉ Maze, Lisburn, Co Down
☎ 028 9262 1256

Horse Riding

The affinity between the Irish and horses is legendary, and there are hundreds of places around the country where you can enjoy lovely scenery on horseback. For further information contact:

Association of Irish Riding Establishments (AIRE)
✉ 11 Moore Park, Newbridge, Co Kildare ☎ 045-431584

Rugby

International Rugby Football Board
✉ Huguenot House 35-38 St Stephens, Dublin 2
☎ 01-2409200

Lansdowne Road
Soak up the atmosphere of a major tournament at this famous ground, which also hosts concerts.
✉ Lansdowne Road Stadium, Ballsbridge ☎ 01-6684601

Soccer

Football Association of Ireland
✉ 80 Merrion Square South, Dublin 2 ☎ 01-7037500

The Irish Football League
✉ Belfast ☎ 028 9024 2888

Fishing
Ireland is one of the outstanding angling destinations in Europe. The variety of venues – sea, river and lake – and types of fish in Irish waters are second to none. There are opportunities for beginners and experts alike and information of all aspects of angling can be found on the website of Central Fisheries Board at www.cfb.ie

What's On When

Irish Celebrations

There are many festivals and events staged throughout Ireland ranging from horse-racing to story-telling. Almost all involve music of some sort, often traditional, and all will guarantee you a day of fun. Opposite is a month-by-month selection of some of the major events held in the Republic and Northern Ireland. For further information and precise dates, contact the local tourist office.

February
Folk Festival, Gleneagles Hotel, Killarney, Co Kerry.

March
Dublin Film Festival.
St Patrick's Day – various pilgrimages and parades.

April
Irish Grand National, Fairyhouse Racecourse.
World Irish Dancing Championship, various locations.

April/May
Beltane Festival, Dingle.

May
Fleadh Nua, Ennis, Co Clare.
Belfast Civic Festival and Lord Mayor's Show.
Balitmore Seafood and Wooden Boat Festival, Baltimore, Co Cork.
Slieve Bloom Walking Festival, Kinnitty, Co Offaly.
The Balmoral Show, Balmoral, Belfast.
The Cathedral Quarter Arts Festival, Belfast.

June
Limavady Jazz and Blues Festival.
Ulster Proms.
Londonderry Walled City Cultural Trail, Londonderry, Co Londonderry.

July
Festival of the Erne, Belturbet, Co Cavan.
Galway Arts Festival.
Boyle Arts Festival, Boyle, Co Roscommon.
Historic Sham Fight, Scarva, Co Down.
Independence Day Celebrations, Ulster American Folk Park, Co Tyrone.

August
Ballyshannon International Folk Festival, Ballyshannon, Co Donegal.
Rose of Tralee Festival, Tralee, Co Kerry.
All Ireland Music Festival, various locations.
Puck Fair, Killorglin, Co Kerry.
Killarney Arts Festival, Co Kerry.

September
Clarenbridge Oyster Festival, Clarenbridge, Co Galway.
Galway International Oyster Festival, Co Galway.
Story Telling Festival, Cape Clear, Co Cork.
Listowel Races, Listowel, Co Kerry.
Appalachian and Blue Grass Festival, Ulster American Folk Park, Co Tyrone.
Waterford International Festival of Light Opera, Waterford, Co Waterford.
Proms in the Park, Donegall Square, Belfast.

October
Dublin Theatre Festival and Fringe Festival.
Cork Jazz Festival.
Cork Film Festival.
Kinsale Gourmet Festival, Co Cork.
Wexford Opera Festival, Wexford, Co Wexford.
Belfast Festival at Queen's.

November
Foyle Film Festival, Londonderry, Co Londonderry.
Listowel Food Fair, Listwowel, Co Kerry.

December
Cinemagic Film Festival, Belfast.

Practical Matters

The following abbreviations
have been used in this section:
NI   Northern Ireland
RI   Republic of Ireland

Above: *Celtic crosses, Inishmore,
Aran Islands*
Right: *Iron way-marker near National
Stud, Kildare*

TIME DIFFERENCES

GMT
12 noon

Ireland
12 noon

Germany
1PM

USA (NY)
7AM

Netherlands
1PM

Spain
1PM

BEFORE YOU GO

WHAT YOU NEED

● Required
○ Suggested
▲ Not required

Passports should be valid for at least six months beyond the date of entry. UK visitors do not need a passport to enter Northern Ireland, but airlines and ferries may insist on it as a form of ID.

	UK	Germany	USA	Netherlands	Spain
Passport/National Identity Card	●	●	●	●	●
Visa (regulations can change – check before booking your journey)	▲	▲	▲	▲	▲
Onward or Return Ticket	○	○	○	○	○
Health Inoculations	▲	▲	▲	▲	▲
Health Documentation (➤ 123, Health)	●	●	●	●	●
Travel Insurance	○	○	○	○	○
Driving Licence (national with English translation, or International)	●	●	●	●	●
Car Insurance Certificate	●	●	●	●	●

WHEN TO GO

Dublin

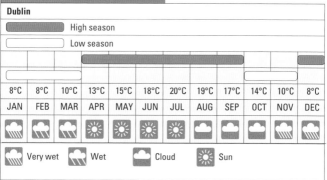

| ▭ | High season |
| ▭ | Low season |

8°C	8°C	10°C	13°C	15°C	18°C	20°C	19°C	17°C	14°C	10°C	8°C
JAN	FEB	MAR	APR	MAY	JUN	JUL	AUG	SEP	OCT	NOV	DEC

Very wet   Wet   Cloud   Sun

TOURIST OFFICES

In the UK
Tourism Ireland
(for Republic &
Northern Ireland)
1 Lower Regent
Street
London SW1Y 4XT

☎ 08000 397000
Fax: 020 7493 906
www.tourism
ireland.com

In the USA
Tourism Ireland
(for Republic &
Northern Ireland)
345 Park Avenue
New York
NY 10154

☎ 212/418 0800
Fax: 212/371 9052

POLICE 999	
FIRE 999	
AMBULANCE 999	
COASTAL RESCUE 999	

WHEN YOU ARE THERE

ARRIVING

Scheduled flights operate from Britain, mainland Europe and North America to Dublin, Cork, Knock, Shannon and Belfast. The Republic's national airline is Aer Lingus (☎ 0870 876 5000). Most ferry services from Britain arrive at Dun Laoghaire and Belfast.

Dublin Airport
Kilometres to city centre

11 kilometres

Journey times

	N/A
	30 minutes
	20 minutes

Belfast Airport
Kilometres to city centre

31 kilometres

Journey times

	60 minutes
	45 minutes
	45 minutes

MONEY

The monetary units are (in the Republic), the euro, and (in Northern Ireland) the pound sterling (£). These are not interchangeable.
On 1 January 2002 the Republic of Ireland adopted the euro and the Irish punt has been withdrawn.
Euro notes (examples shown) come in denominations of 500, 200, 100, 50, 20, 10 and 5; coins in denominations of 2 and 1 euros, 50, 20, 10, 5, 2 and 1 cents.

Pounds Sterling notes for Northern Ireland are issued by the Bank of England in denominations of 50, 20, 10 and 5; coins in denominations of £2 and £1, 50, 20, 10, 5, 2 and 1 pence.
Provincial banks also issue notes in denominations of 50, 20, 10 and 5 (examples shown), but these are not accepted in other parts of the UK.

TIME

Ireland observes Greenwich Mean Time (GMT), but from late March, when clocks are put forward one hour, until late October, summer time (GMT +1) operates.

CUSTOMS

YES
From another EU country for personal use (guidelines)
800 cigarettes, 200 cigars, 1 kilogram of tobacco
10 litres of spirits (over 22%)
20 litres of aperitifs
90 litres of wine, of which 60 litres can be sparkling wine
110 litres of beer

From a non-EU country for your personal use, the allowances are:
200 cigarettes OR
50 cigars OR 250 grams of tobacco
1 litre of spirits (over 22%)
2 litres of intermediary products (eg sherry) and sparkling wine
2 litres of still wine
50 grams of perfume
0.25 litres of eau de toilette
The value limit for goods is 175 euros

Travellers under 17 years of age are not entitled to the tobacco and alcohol allowances.

NO
Drugs, firearms, ammunition, offensive weapons, obscene material, unlicensed animals.

EMBASSIES

UK
01-205 3700

Germany
020 7824 1300 (NI)
01-269 3011 (RI)

USA
028 9032 8239 (NI)
01-668 8777 (RI)

Netherlands
028 9077 9088 (NI)
01-269 3444 (RI)

Spain
028 9070 9348 (NI)
01-283 9900 (RI)

WHEN YOU ARE THERE

TOURIST OFFICES

Republic of Ireland

- Dublin Tourism
  Suffolk Street, Dublin 2
  ☎ 01-605 7700
  www.dublin.com

- Southeast Tourism
  41 The Quay, Waterford
  ☎ 051-875788
  www.southeastireland.com

- Cork-Kerry Tourism
  Grand Parade, Cork City
  ☎ 021-4255100
  www.corkkerry.ie

- Shannon Development
  Tourism Division, Shannon
  Town Centre, Co Clare
  ☎ 061-361555
  www.shannon-dev.ie

- Ireland West Tourism
  Forster Street, Galway City
  ☎ 091-537700
  www.irelandwest.ie

- Northwest Tourism
  Temple Street, Sligo
  ☎ 071-916 1201
  www.irelandnorthwest.ie

- East Coast & Midlands
  Tourism
  Clonard House, Dublin Rd,
  Mullingar, Co Westmeath
  ☎ 044-48650
  www.eastcoast
  midlandsireland.com

Northern Ireland

- Tourist Information Centre
  St Anne's Court, 59 North
  Street, Belfast BT1 1NB
  ☎ 028 9023 1221
  www.discover
  northernireland.com

NATIONAL HOLIDAYS

J	F	M	A	M	J	J	A	S	O	N	D
1		1(3)	(2)	2	1	1	2		1		2

1 Jan	New Year's Day
17 Mar	St Patrick's Day
Mar/Apr	Good Friday, Easter Monday
May (1st Mon)	May Holiday
May (last Mon)	Spring Holiday (NI)
Jun (1st Mon)	June Holiday (RI)
12 Jul	Orangeman's Day (NI)
Aug (1st Mon)	August Holiday (RI)
Aug (last Mon)	Late Summer Holiday (NI)
Oct (last Mon)	October Holiday (RI)
25 Dec	Christmas Day
26 Dec	St Stephen's Day

OPENING HOURS

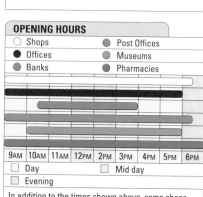

○ Shops   ● Post Offices
● Offices   ● Museums
● Banks   ● Pharmacies

□ Day   □ Mid day
□ Evening

In addition to the times shown above, some shops stay open till 8 or 9PM for late-night shopping on Thursday and Friday. Smaller towns and rural areas have an early closing day on one day a week. Nearly all banks are closed on Saturday and many post offices close at 1PM.

The opening times of museums and tourist sites vary and are subject to change; always check with a local tourist office. Many places close from October to March or have very limited opening, although most major sights are open all year.

120

DRIVE ON THE LEFT

TOILETS FREE

PUBLIC TRANSPORT

Internal Flights Flights from Dublin to other airports in Ireland are operated by Aer Lingus (☎ 0870 876 5000 and Ryanair (☎ 0871 246 0000). Aer Arann (in Ireland ☎ 01-8447700) operates the Aran Flyer with several daily flights between the Aran Islands and Galway.

Trains In the Republic a limited network run by Iarnród Éireann (☎ 01-7032358) serves major towns and cities. Trains are comfortable, generally reliable and fares reasonable. Northern Ireland Railways (☎ 028 9066 6630) operates services from Belfast to main towns and to Dublin.

Long Distance Buses In the Republic, Bus Éireann (☎ 01-836 6111) operates a network of express bus routes serving most of the country (some run summer only). In Northern Ireland, Ulsterbus (☎ 028 9066 6630), has links between Belfast and most villages and towns. Unlimited travel tickets are available.

Ferries Two car ferries operate between Ballyhack, Co Wexford and Passage East, Co Waterford (☎ 051-382480) and Killimer, Co Clare and Tarbert, Co Kerry (☎ 065 905 3124), the latter saving 100km on the road journey. There are also ferry services from the mainland to some islands.

Urban Transport City bus services, particularly in Dublin and Belfast, are excellent. Dublin is served by Dublin Bus (☎ 01873 4222) and also has a Rapid Transit system (DART). A 4-day ticket is available, covering bus and train travel, too. Citybus (☎ 028 9066 6630) serves the Belfast area.

CAR RENTAL

All of the international car rental firms are represented. A car from a local company, however, is likely to offer cheaper rates, but may not allow different pick-up/drop-off points. Car rental is also less expensive in Northern Ireland than in the Republic.

TAXIS

Taxis are available in major towns and cities, at taxi stands or outside hotels, and at main rail stations, ports and airports. In Belfast, black cabs may be shared by customers and some operate rather like buses, shuttling their passengers between the city and the suburbs.

DRIVING

Speed limits on motorways and dual carriageways: **112kph/70mph**

Speed limits on country roads: **96kph/60mph**

Speed limits on urban roads: **48kph/30mph (or as signposted)**

Must be worn in front seats at all times and in rear seats where fitted.

Random breath-testing. Never drive under the influence of alcohol.

Lead replacement petrol (LRP) and unleaded petrol are widely available on both sides of the border. Fuel stations in villages in the Republic stay open until 8 or 9PM, and open after Mass on Sundays. In Northern Ireland, 24-hour petrol stations are fairly common. Fuel is cheaper in Northern Ireland than in the Republic.

If you break down driving your own car and are a member of an AIT-affiliated motoring club, you can call the Automobile Association's rescue service (☎ 1800 667788 in the Republic; ☎ 0800 887766 in Northern Ireland). If the car is rented follow the instructions given in the documentation; most of the international rental firms provide a rescue service.

PERSONAL SAFETY

The national police forces are:

RI – Garda Síochána (pronounced *sheekawnah*) in black-and-blue uniforms

NI – Royal Ulster Constabulary (RUC) in dark green uniforms.

- Be wary in suburban areas of Belfast, southern Co Armagh and Coalisland, Co Tyrone, which are prone to sectarian violence.
- Take care of personal property in Dublin.
- Avoid leaving property visible in cars.

Police assistance:
☎ **999**
from any call box

TELEPHONES

Public telephone boxes, blue and grey in the Republic and red in Northern Ireland, are being replaced by glass and metal booths. To make a call, lift the handset, insert the correct coins (RI: 10, 20 or 50 cents, or €1; NI: 10, 20 or 50 pence, or £1) or phonecard and dial.

International Dialling Codes

From Ireland to:

UK:	**00 44** (RI only; no code needed from NI)
Germany:	**00 49**
USA:	**00 1**
Netherlands:	**00 31**
Spain:	**00 34**

POST

RI   NI

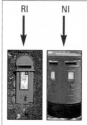

Post Offices
The main post offices in O'Connell Street, Dublin, and Castle Place, Belfast, are open extended hours, otherwise hours are:
Open: 9AM
Closed: 5:30PM (Sat: 1PM/RI, 12:30PM/NI)
☎ 01-705 7000 (RI)
☎ 028 9032 3740 (NI)

ELECTRICITY

The native power supply is: 230 volts (RI); 240 volts (NI)

Type of socket: 3 square-pin (UK type). Parts of the Republic also have 2 round-pin (continental type).
Overseas visitors should bring a good travel adaptor.

TIPS/GRATUITIES

Yes ✓ No ✗		
Restaurants (if service not included)	✓	10%
Cafés (if service not included)	✓	10%
Hotels (if service not included)	✓	10%
Hairdressers	✓	£1/€2
Taxis	✓	10%
Tour guides	✓	£1/€2
Cinema usherettes	✗	
Porters	✓	50p/€1
Cloakroom attendants	✓	50p/€1
Toilets	✗	

PHOTOGRAPHY

Best times to photograph: early morning and late evening. Irish light can be dull so you may need faster film eg 200 or 400 ASA.
Where to buy film: film and camera batteries are readily available in many shops and pharmacies.
Restrictions: in Northern Ireland you cannot photograph inside museums or take photographs of military installations, vehicles or personnel.

HEALTH

Insurance

Nationals of EU and certain other countries can get discounted medical treatment in Ireland with the European Health Insurance Card (not required for UK nationals). Private medical insurance is still advised and is essential for all other visitors.

Dental Services

Nationals of EU and certain other countries can get discounted dental treatment within the Irish health service with the European Health Insurance Card (not needed for UK nationals). Others should take out private medical insurance.

Sun Advice

The sunniest months are May and June with on average 5–6½ hours of sun a day (the extreme southeast is the sunniest), though July and August are the hottest. During these months you should take the normal precautions against the sun.

Drugs

Prescription and non-prescription drugs and medicines are available from pharmacies. When closed, most display on their doors the address of the nearest one open. In an emergency, contact the nearest hospital.

Safe Water

Tap water in Ireland is perfectly safe to drink. However, if you prefer to drink bottled water you will find it widely available.

CONCESSIONS

Students Holders of an International Student Identity Card can buy a Travelsave Stamp which entitles them to travel discounts including a 50 per cent reduction on Bus Éireann, Iarnród Éireann and Irish Ferries (between Britain and Ireland). Contact your local student travel agency for further details. The Travelsave Stamp can be purchased from USIT, 19–21 Aston Quay, O'Connell Bridge, Dublin 2 (☎ 01-6021904).

Senior Citizens Many car rental companies give discounts to those over 50 or 55, as do some hotels and a few tourist attractions. Some tour companies offer special spring and autumn package deals.

CLOTHING SIZES

Ireland	UK	Rest of Europe	USA	
36	36	46	36	Suits
38	38	48	38	Suits
40	40	50	40	Suits
42	42	52	42	Suits
44	44	54	44	Suits
46	46	56	46	Suits
7	7	41	8	Shoes
7.5	7.5	42	8.5	Shoes
8.5	8.5	43	9.5	Shoes
9.5	9.5	44	10.5	Shoes
10.5	10.5	45	11.5	Shoes
11	11	46	12	Shoes
14.5	14.5	37	14.5	Shirts
15	15	38	15	Shirts
15.5	15.5	39/40	15.5	Shirts
16	16	41	16	Shirts
16.5	16.5	42	16.5	Shirts
17	17	43	17	Shirts
8	8	34	6	Dresses
10	10	36	8	Dresses
12	12	38	10	Dresses
14	14	40	12	Dresses
16	16	42	14	Dresses
18	18	44	16	Dresses
4.5	4.5	38	6	Shoes
5	5	38	6.5	Shoes
5.5	5.5	39	7	Shoes
6	6	39	7.5	Shoes
6.5	6.5	40	8	Shoes
7	7	41	8.5	Shoes

LANGUAGE

The Republic has two official languages, English and Irish. Everyone speaks English, though you are likely to hear Irish in the Gaeltacht areas of the west and south (Kerry, Galway, Mayo, the Aran Islands, Donegal and Ring, and Co Waterford), where you may find road signs in Irish only. Irish is a Celtic language, probably introduced to Ireland by the Celts in the last few centuries BC. Below is a list of some words that you may come across whilst in Ireland, with a guide to pronunciation.

hotel	*óstán*	*(oh stawn)*
bed and breakfast	*loistín oíche*	*(lowshteen eeheh)*
single room	*seomra singil*	*(showmra shingle)*
double room	*seomra dúbailte*	*(showmra dhubillta)*
one person	*aon duine*	*(ayn dinnah)*
one night	*oíche amháin*	*(eeheh a waa-in)*
chambermaid	*cailín aimsire*	*(colleen eym-shir-eh)*
room service	*seirbhís seomraí*	*(sher-iv-eeesh showm-ree)*

bank	*an banc*	*(an bonk)*
exchange office	*oifig malairte*	*(if-ig moll-ir-teh)*
post office	*oifig an phoist*	*(if-ig on fwisht)*
coin	*bonn*	*(bown)*
banknote	*nóta bainc*	*(no-tah bank)*
cheque	*seic*	*(sheck)*
travellers' cheque	*seic taistil*	*(sheck tash-till)*
credit card	*cárta creidmheasa*	*(korta kred-vassa)*

restaurant	*bialann*	*(bee-a-lunn)*
café	*caife*	*(koff-ay)*
pub/bar	*tábhairne*	*(thaw-ir-neh)*
breakfast	*bricfeásta*	*(brick-faw-stah)*
lunch	*lón*	*(lone)*
dinner	*dinnéar*	*(dinn-air)*
table	*tábla*	*(thaw-blah)*
waiter	*freastalaí*	*(frass-tol-ee)*

aeroplane	*eitleán*	*(ett-ell-awn)*
airport	*aerfort*	*(air-furt)*
train	*traein*	*(train)*
bus	*bus*	*(bus)*
station	*stáisiún*	*(staw-shoon)*
boat	*bád*	*(bawd)*
port	*port*	*(purt)*
ticket	*ticéad*	*(tickaid)*

yes	*tá/sea*	*(thaw/shah)*
no	*níl/ní hea*	*(knee hah)*
please	*le do thoil*	*(le do hull)*
thank you	*go raibh maith aguth*	*(goh rev moh aguth)*
welcome	*fáilte*	*(fawl-che)*
hello	*dia dhuit*	*(dee-a-gwit)*
goodbye	*slán*	*(slawn)*
goodnight	*oíche mhaith*	*(eeheh woh)*
excuse me	*gabh mo leithscéal*	*(gov-mu-le-schale)*
how much?	*cé mhéid?*	*(kay vaid)*
open/closed	*oscailte/dúnta*	*(uskulta/doonta)*

Acknowledgements
The Automobile Association wishes to thank the following libraries, photographers and associations for their assistance in the preparation of this book:
MARY EVANS PICTURE LIBRARY 10/11; CHRIS HILL 20/1, 56; MRI BANKERS' GUIDE TO FOREIGN CURRENCY 119; NATIONAL MUSEUM OF IRELAND 24; NORTHERN IRELAND TOURIST BOARD 85, 86, 87; www.euro.ecb.int 119 (euro notes).
The remaining pictures are from the Association's own library (AA PHOTO LIBRARY) with contributions from:
JAMIE BLANDFORD 5a, 12, 15a, 19, 23, 27a, 46, 54, 59; LIAM BRADY 12/13, 15b, 36, 42, 69, 70, 83; STEVE DAY 1, 33, 37, 38, 44, 63, 68, 71; MICHAEL DIGGIN 5b, 53, 90, 122a/b/c; DEREK FORSS 51; CHRIS HILL 6, 60, 64, 82; STEFAN HILL 2, 9b, 16, 27b, 49, 52, 55, 73, 91a, 117a; JILL JOHNSON 8; CAROLINE JONES 51; TOM KELLY 7; GEORGE MUNDAY 26, 72, 76, 77, 79, 80, 81, 84, 88, 89; MICHAEL SHORT 18, 22, 30, 39, 40, 43, 45, 57a, 61, 91b, 117b; SLIDE FILE 35, 41; PETER ZOLLER 17, 25, 66, 67

Author's Acknowledgements
Penny Phenix would like to thank Terry Arsenault, her husband and business partner, for invaluable assistance with the walks and drives, for additional research and checking; also to acknowledge the assistance of Borde Fáilte, the Northern Ireland Tourist Board, various tourist offices throughout Ireland and Charleville Lodge in Dublin.

Contributors
Copy editor: Pat Pierce Page Layout: Design 23 Indexer: Marie Lorimer
Updated by Apostrophe S Limited

Dear Essential Traveller

Your comments, opinions and recommendations are very important to us. So please help us to improve our travel guides by taking a few minutes to complete this simple questionnaire.

You do not need a stamp (unless posted outside the UK). If you do not want to cut this page from your guide, then photocopy it or write your answers on a plain sheet of paper.

Send to: **The Editor, AA World Travel Guides, FREEPOST SCE 4598, Basingstoke RG21 4GY.**

Your recommendations...

We always encourage readers' recommendations for restaurants, nightlife or shopping – if your recommendation is used in the next edition of the guide, we will send you a *FREE* AA *Essential* Guide of your choice. Please state below the establishment name, location and your reasons for recommending it.

_____

_____

_____

_____

Please send me **AA *Essential*** _____

About this guide...

Which title did you buy?

AA *Essential* _____

Where did you buy it?_____

When? m m / y y

Why did you choose an AA *Essential* Guide? _____

_____

_____

_____

_____

Did this guide meet your expectations?

Exceeded ☐ Met all ☐ Met most ☐ Fell below ☐

Please give your reasons_____

_____

_____

_____

continued on next page...

Were there any aspects of this guide that you particularly liked? _____

_____

_____

Is there anything we could have done better? _____

_____

_____

About you...

Name (*Mr/Mrs/Ms*) _____

Address _____

_____

_____ Postcode _____

Daytime tel nos _____

Please only give us your mobile phone number if you wish to hear from us about other products and services from the AA and partners by text or mms.

Which age group are you in?

Under 25 ☐ 25–34 ☐ 35–44 ☐ 45–54 ☐ 55–64 ☐ 65+ ☐

How many trips do you make a year?

Less than one ☐ One ☐ Two ☐ Three or more ☐

Are you an AA member? Yes ☐ No ☐

About your trip...

When did you book? m m / y y   When did you travel? m m / y y

How long did you stay? _____

Was it for business or leisure? _____

Did you buy any other travel guides for your trip?

If yes, which ones? _____

Thank you for taking the time to complete this questionnaire. Please send it to us as soon as possible, and remember, you do not need a stamp (*unless posted outside the UK*).

Happy Holidays!

The Atlas

Acknowledgements
All pictures are from AA World Travel Library with contributions from the following photographers:
Stephen Whitehorn: O'Connell Street, Dublin, children on horseback
Michael Short: pub musicians
Derek Forss: the River Liffey, Dublin
George Munday: Giants Causeway
Steve Day: café life

Day One

Day Two

Day Three

Day Four

Day Five

Day Six

Day Seven

The Automobile Association
www.theAA.com
The Automobile Association's website offers comprehensive and up-to-the-minute
information covering AA-approved hotels, guest houses and B&Bs, restaurants and
pubs in the UK; airport parking, insurance, European breakdown cover, European
motoring advice, a ferry planner, European route planner, overseas fuel prices, a
bookshop and much more.

The Foreign and Commonwealth Office
Country advice, traveller's tips, before you
go information, checklists and more.
www.fco.gov.uk

Republic of Ireland
www.ireland.ie
www.southeastireland.com
www.corkkerry.ie
www.shannon-dev.ie
www.irelandwest.ie
www.irelandnorthwest.ie
www.eastcoastmidlandsireland.com

Northern Ireland
www.discovernorthernireland.com

GENERAL
UK Passport Service
www.ukpa.gov.uk

Health Advice for Travellers
www.doh.gov.uk/traveladvice

UK Travel Insurance Directory
www.uktravelinsurancedirectory.co.uk

BBC – Holiday
www.bbc.co.uk/holiday

The Full Universal Currency Converter
www.xe.com/ucc/full.shtml

Flying with Kids
www.flyingwithkids.com

TRAVEL
Flights and Information
www.cheapflights.co.uk
www.thisistravel.co.uk
www.ba.com
www.worldairportguide.com

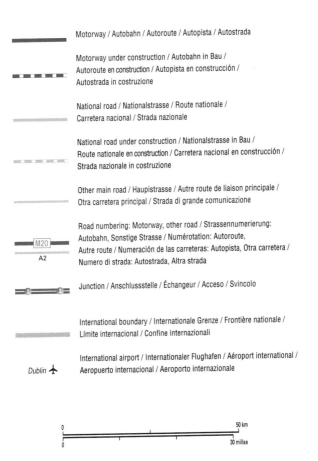

Motorway / Autobahn / Autoroute / Autopista / Autostrada

Motorway under construction / Autobahn in Bau / Autoroute en construction / Autopista en construcción / Autostrada in costruzione

National road / Nationalstrasse / Route nationale / Carretera nacional / Strada nazionale

National road under construction / Nationalstrasse in Bau / Route nationale en construction / Carretera nacional en construcción / Strada nazionale in costruzione

Other main road / Haupistrasse / Autre route de liaison principale / Otra carretera principal / Strada di grande comunicazione

Road numbering: Motorway, other road / Strassennumerierung: Autobahn, Sonstige Strasse / Numérotation: Autoroute, Autre route / Numeración de las carreteras: Autopista, Otra carretera / Numero di strada: Autostrada, Altra strada

Junction / Anschlussstelle / Échangeur / Acceso / Svincolo

International boundary / Internationale Grenze / Frontière nationale / Límite internacional / Confine internazionali

International airport / Internationaler Flughafen / Aéroport international / Aeropuerto internacional / Aeroporto internazionale

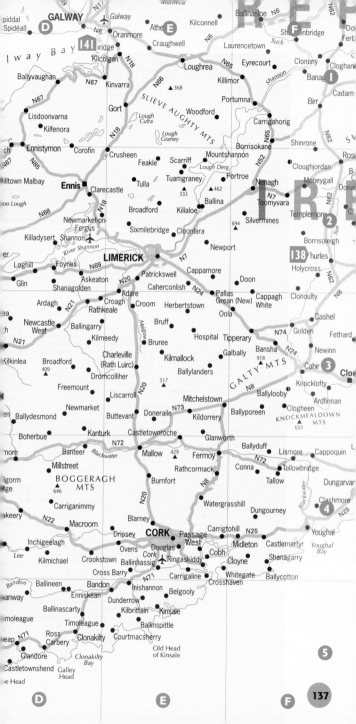

Termonfeckin

Drogheda

ane

[M1] **143**

uleek Ardcath Balbriggan
ristown Naul Balrothery
  Skerries
Lusk Rush
ath Ashbourne Portrane Lambay
  N2 Island
Dublin Malahide
Dunboyne Portmarnock
Leixlip Howth
  6 Toll
alkin Lucan N7
Tallaght 10
  11
DUBLIN
Brittas **Dun Laoghaire**
  M50
  Killiney
essington [M11] Bray
Poulaphouca Kilmacanoge
Reservoir Greystones
848 N11
AGHCLEEVAUN Roundwood Kilcoole
  Newtownmountkennedy

KLOW
ndalough Ashford
  27 Rathnew
S TABLE Laragh Wicklow
T S Glenealy *Wicklow Head*
Rathdrum

  Brittas Bay
Aughrim Avoca
  Mizen Head
  Woodenbridge
Tinahely N11 **Arklow**

arnew *Kilmichael Point*
Gorey
  Courtown
  Harbour

Ballycanew
  Cahore Point
rns

orthy

Blackwater

te
Curracloe
  Wexford or
  North Bay
Wexford
  Rosslare
  Rosslare Harbour
Tagoat
vn

Carnsore Point

ds

I

2

3

4

5

A   B   C

1

2

Erris Head   *Broad Haven*

Belmullet
(Béal an Mhuirhead)

Inishkea North   Bunnahowen

Inishkea South

Duvillaun More   *Blacksod Bay*

Achill Head   672
SLIEVE MORE

Achill Island   Keel

Carrowmore *Lake*

Bangor Erris

N59

722 ▲

Lough Feeagh

3

Mulrany   Newp

Clare Island   *Clew Bay*

Westport

Inishturk   Louisburgh   ▲ CROAGH PATRICK 765

Caher Island

Inishbofin

Inishshark

4

N59

673 ▲

Leenane   Clonbur
(An Fhairc

Letterfrack

Clifden   Cornamona

Mannin Bay   N59

Ballyconneely

Slyne Head   Roundstone

Croaghnakeela Island   Glinsk
(Glinsce)

Ought

Kilkieran

5

Gorumna Island   Spidd
(An Spid

North Sound

136   Inishmore   G a l

140   A   B   C   Aran Islands   Inishmaan

Ba

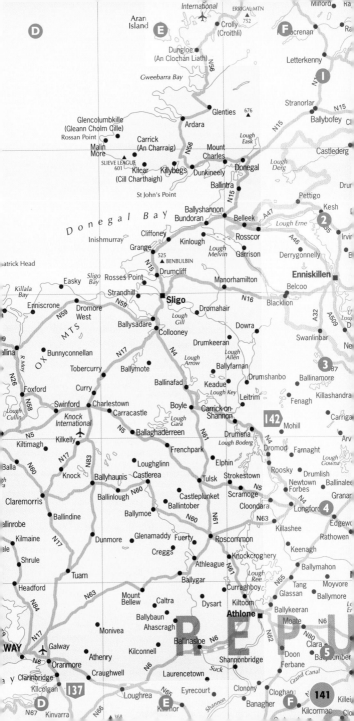

Rathlin
Island

White Park Bay

Bushmills

Ballycastle

Dervock

Armoy

Red Bay
Garron Point

Ballymoney

Cushendall

Dunloy

Carnlough   Glenarm

Rasharkin   A43

A26

Culleybackey   M2   Broughshane

Ballygalley

one   Ballymena   Ballygalley Head

duff   Ahoghill   Moorfields   Larne

ERN   Kells   A36   Island Magee

Bellaghy   A26   M2   Ballyclare   Ballycarry

Randalstown   Doagh   Ballynure   Whitehead

Ballyronan   Antrim   Carrickfergus

Belfast   Newtownabbey

International   M5   Bangor

own   Lough   Crumlin   BELFAST   Donaghadee

Neagh   Glenavy   Holywood   A48

A N D   *Belfast City*   Newtownards

Lisburn   Dunmurry   A23   Comber

M1   A501   Carryduff   Ballywalter

Mazetown   A24   Ballygowan   Greyabbey

Lurgan   Saintfield   Kircubbin

Craigavon   Hillsborough   *Strangford Lough*   Portavogie

Gilford   Dromore   A49   Killyleagh

agee   Banbridge   Ballynahinch   Portaferry

.51   Scarva   Strangford

ll   A27   Loughbrickland   Clough   A25   Downpatrick

Poyntzpass   A50   Castlewellan   Dundrum   Ardglass

Rathfriland   A25   Maghera   Killough

A25   Hilltown   852   Newcastle   St John's Point

Newry   MOURNE

A28   MTS

Warrenpoint   A2   Annalong

urry   Omeath   Rostrevor   Kilkeel

N1   Carlingford

Dundalk

Dundalk Bay

Castlebellingham

M1   Dunany Point

dee   Dunleer

Termonfeckin

Drogheda

ne   M1   139

leek   Ardcath   Balbriggan

istown   Naul   Balrothery

Skerries

Sight Locator Index

This index relates to the atlas section on pages 136–43. We have given map references to the main sights of interest in the book. Some sights in the index may not be plotted on the atlas.

For the main index see pages 125–26